100

NATURE
Verbe Nature
WORD

R.A. Schwaller de Lubicz, Plan de Grasse, c. 1960
(Photographie Appollot, Grasse)

NATURE
Verbe Nature
WORD

R.A. Schwaller de Lubicz

*Translated from the French
by Deborah Lawlor*

INNER TRADITIONS INTERNATIONAL
Rochester, Vermont

Inner Traditions International, Ltd.
One Park Street
Rochester, Vermont 05767

First Inner Traditions edition 1990

First published as *Verbe Nature* in
"Aor," R.A. Schwaller de Lubicz, Sa vie — Son oeuvre
by La Colombe, Paris 1963;
©R.A. Schwaller de Lubicz 1961

Translation copyright © Deborah Lawlor 1982
All rights reserved

Library of Congress Cataloging-in-Publication Data

Schwaller de Lubicz, R.A.
[Verbe nature. English]
Nature word = Verbe nature / R.A. Schwaller de Lubicz ; translated
from the French by Deborah Lawlor. — 1st Inner Traditions ed.
p.   cm.
Translation of Verbe nature.
Reprint. Originally published: West Stockbridge, Mass.:
Lindisfarne Press, 1982.
Includes bibliographical references.
ISBN 0-89281-036-X
1. Nature — Miscellanea.   2. Hermeticism.   I. Title.
[BF1999.S361913 1990]
135'.4--dc20   90-30903
                                                         CIP

Printed and bound in the United States of America

10   9   8   7   6   5   4   3   2

Distributed to the book trade in Canada by
Book Center, Inc., Montreal, Quebec

The publisher gratefully acknowledges the help of
Mlle. Lucie Lamy

Contents

Foreword

Nature Word,
the Hermetic Tradition, and Today

Hermes saw the totality of things. Having seen, he understood. Having understood, he had the power to reveal and show. And indeed what he knew, he wrote down. What he wrote, he mostly hid away, keeping silence rather than speaking out, so that every generation on coming into the world had to seek out these things.

> —*Kore Kosmou* (*The Virgin of the World*)

So go, then, my child, to a certain labourer and ask him what he has sown and what he has harvested, and you will learn from him that the man who sows wheat also harvests wheat, and the man who sows barley also harvests barley. . . . Learn to comprehend the whole fabrication, *demiourgia*, and generation of things and know that it is the condition of man to sow a man, of a lion to sow a lion, of a dog to sow a dog. . . . See, there is the whole of the mystery.

> —Isis the Prophetess to her Son Horus

And he said unto them, Go ye into all the world, and preach the gospel to every creature.

> —Mark, 16:15

IT IS DIFFICULT to know how to present *Nature Word* to the unprepared reader. Certainly it is a work of the greatest passion, seriousness and authority, and never for a moment do we suspect that the author is merely speculating; on the contrary, he continually convinces us that he has lived what he teaches — so much so, indeed, that in reading his work we feel privy to an act of testimony or witness, that the author has seen and knows and now must tell what he has seen. From this point of view, *Nature Word* could be called a prophetic text; yet, paradoxically, it is completely contemporary and speaks directly to the needs and concerns of our time. None of this is usual today — we like to keep separate what *Nature Word* combines — and so, as is the author's intention, we are never sure whether his work is primarily religious, philosophical or scientific. In fact, it is all three in equal measure.

Taking mystery and the spiritual life for granted and as its starting point, *Nature Word* uses theological and mythological language where necessary, and yet argues philosophically, logically, forcing us to think in ways that we are quite unused to; then, stranger still perhaps, it returns repeatedly to the meaning and explanation of the natural world, with a respect for detail usually thought of as scientific, but which in this case is really religious, that is, founded on mystery. And so it goes, round and round; nor is this circularity limited to the argument and its language, for it soon becomes evident that the author believes that it is in the very nature of the universe, Ourobouros-like, to be circular, a nonexteriorized whole of which every part is connected to every other part. To comprehend this universe and our place in it, so the author claims, we must learn to think without objectifying. Hence his work begins as epistemology, continues as ontology, and concludes as injunction, setting forth what the reader must do to see for himself what the author has seen.

There are thus many different ways of approaching

Nature Word, but perhaps the most appropriate would be as a Hermetic work of Christian philosophy or, taking philosophy in its original sense as a "Way," of esoteric Christianity. Thereby *Nature Word* takes its place in an august tradition, whose antiquity and consistency through diverse times and contexts serve to remind us both of our roots and of the fact that it is we, rather than it, who are unusual and require explanation. Indeed, as its cosmological and thereby scientific aspect, the so-called Hermetic tradition is an integral part of our cultural heritage. Given then that *Nature Word* is of the Hermetic tradition, that this tradition is central to our history and that we have forgotten it, there is perhaps no better way to approach Schwaller de Lubicz's testimony than with a mind newly familiarized with Hermetic teaching and practice.

Deriving principally from Egypt and sharing a certain commonality of origin with Pythagoreanism, Platonism, Neo-Platonism and some manifestations of gnosticism—not to mention Kabbalah and the Mosaic Teachings of the Old Testament—the Hermetic tradition became, during the last two thousand years, the natural complement of the Christian Revelation. Christianity, as theology and history, needed a cosmology or sacred, Hermetic, idea of nature for its complete embodiment, while Hermeticism, for its part, found in the Christ not only the initiatic effusion necessary for its survival but also its supernatural justification and natural consummation. As cosmology, Hermeticism required a ground from which to derive and a goal toward which to aspire, a Mystery; and the Christian Mystery as revealed by the Trinity (and the Incarnation) was providential in providing this, because the revelation of Christ unveiled the Human Mystery while it was the "human" world which was precisely also the Hermetic or cosmological one, mediating and reconciling celestial and terrestrial realms. From this point of view the Christian Mystery was the revelation of the divinity of Humanity and the Cosmos and so vindicated Hermeticism, which was founded upon just this certitude, as an authentic Christian esotericism or Way. Thus, the Hermetic science of alchemy was to teach that "The Stone is the Christ," celebrating a sacramental science whose object was the divinization of the cosmos, its revelation as the Anthropos whose Resurrection Body was at once the Body of God and the Body of Man.

That such ideals could be dangerous if misunderstood or assimilated without due preparation goes without saying. One may therefore understand the attitude of the Church Fathers in wishing to conceal the truth upon which they were founded. Nevertheless, for whoever has eyes to see, the human mystery of Christ was clearly proclaimed by the Bible, and particularly by St. John and St. Paul. The veil of the Temple had been rent, and lo! Man found himself: the Word in the beginning was revealed to have been made flesh. "And there are others," wrote Irenaeus about certain Valentinians, "who assert that the Forefather of all things himself, the Pre-beginning and Pre-unthinkable, is called 'Man,' and that this is the great and hidden mystery, namely, that the power which is above all and which embraces all is termed Man. And because of this the Saviour designates himself Son of Man."[1]

Modern science, insofar as it is cosmological, is "Hermetic." But, by virtue of its claim to be rationally autonomous and self-constituted, rather than open to, deriving from (and expressive of) Mystery, it is not and must be viewed, from the Hermetic point of view, as a local and temporary loss of orientation, as the perhaps chaotic but nevertheless necessary precondition for a new birth. One may speak here of a mutation of the spirit, of what has been called an epistemological rupture. Scientific method, having trained and developed certain faculties of reasoning, not to mention moral faculties such as "intellectual" rigor and honesty, has reached its limits; and by virtue of the self-contradictions and paradoxes that these limits generate and reveal, it opens the possibility for the development of new faculties of knowing based to some extent upon these very contradictions. The whole movement of thought and philosophy this century has been towards the necessity of learning to think without objectifying and of basing upon such thinking a new theory of truth and a new science. Such a science would once more be true science from a Hermetic point of view, that is, a unifying science of causes, not facts, seeking to penetrate the mystery presiding over material phenomena, rather than objectifying the phenomena themselves into a "system."

In order to understand this as it is intended we must clearly distinguish science and scientific thinking from what is more appropriately called technology and technological thinking. The modern age—"The Age of the World Picture" as Heidegger[2] terms it—represents not so much the ascendancy of science as that of technology and the machine. This is to say that inasmuch as it conditions culture scientific thinking has become technological thinking; the objectification and projection of "nature" as a fixed, self-contained, atomized spatio-temporal picture or system, whose parts operate according to certain abstract, predominantly statistical laws ("the laws of nature"), which are clearly definable (usually in terms of mathematics) and so are verifiable within the projected framework, where they may be manipulated and calculated in terms of work or

15

energy. It is this science of the "picturable" which makes exact research possible and penetrates every level of contemporary life.

What should be noted here is that, in its logic and development, this picture depends entirely upon what is given by the senses (or by mechanical extensions of these). Thus it is organized according to a "sense-based" logic or, rather, according to a logic which, because it is sense-based, has been founded, since Aristotle, upon *the law of contradiction*—that "the same attribute cannot belong and not belong to the same thing at the same time in the same respect"—and *the law of the excluded middle*—that "B cannot both be B and not B"—thereby giving rise to the loneliness and suffering occasioned by the twofold impenetrability of space and time. Nature has become a system, conceivable and graspable as a picture within limits defined by the senses, while truth has become the comforting certainty of the shared representation rather than the disclosure of the Real which is a certainty revealed in the individual soul.

Unfortunately, both what it means to be human in general and more particularly an understanding of the twofold reality of consciousness and matter fall outside these sensory limits and so are not able to be represented within the picture. Here we are up against the consequences referred to by the poet and philosopher Coleridge as "that despotism of the eye" which derives from the assumption that the spatial world exists objectively, whereas in fact the spatial world is projected by the rational consciousness working in isolation from other centers or fields of knowing. Coleridge spoke of "that Slavery of the Mind to the Eye and the visual Imagination or Fancy under the influence of which the Reasoner must have a *picture* and mistakes surface for substance." Such men, he added, "consequently *demand* a

Matter as a *Datum*." However, he continued, "As soon as this gross prejudice is cured by the appropriate discipline and the Mind is familiarised to the contemplation of Matter as a product in time . . . the idea of *Creation* alone remains."[3]

Traditional Hermetic science, based as it was upon such a discipline, was something very different. Rather than having to do with the objectification and control of the known by the knower, it sought to embody a process of unification and identity. The object was conceived of as a symbol: that is, Hermetic science strove for a qualitative, unifying exaltation of the relation of the knower to the known in the symbol through the act of knowing. Knowledge was thus the means by which the human being participated in and contributed to an "evolution," whose end was the coming-into-unity of the whole. Indeed, from many points of view, the human being was none other than the means of this coming-into-unity, just as by the "fall" humanity had embodied and been the means of multiplicity — of unity's unfolding or self-articulation into a multiplicity, not of objects, but of relations. Such unity and multiplicity, however, must not be thought of as opposites but rather as the polarization, in Coleridge's words, of "two forces of one power."

Hermetically, knowledge and evolution are one, and are founded upon the primacy of humanity as life and consciousness. The human being, in other words, finding himself in our world, in a sense-based psychological consciousness of multiplicity — a consciousness that separates — but bearing within himself the memory of original unity — a consciousness of distinction without separation — was called upon to perceive it as his right and duty to gradually

17

transform the one by the other. Science was the way and contemplation of this process. Methodologically, it was a way of posing and articulating this unity, for unless each perception or act unified, "things" (the consciousness that separates) could not be truly understood as interconnected, nor life (*bios*), soul (*psyche*), Nature (*physis*) or man (*anthropos*) understood.

Thus it was the assumption of Hermetic science that the whole universe was sacramental, embodying and proclaiming this process of the revelation of unity—of unity as *identity*, however, rather than as non-duality. The Christian teaching of the Trinity, particularly as contained in the Prologue to the Gospel of St. John, is the key here: "*In the beginning was the Word, and the Word was with God, and the Word was God. The same was in the beginning with God.*" Here the Identity of the Unspeakable Unity is revealed as *mediated*: it is at once Origin, Word and *With* (as a thing that is identical is the same *with respect to* itself, is returned *towards* itself). St. John then goes on to assert, most importantly, that an identity exists also between the innate, total consciousness which is Man, for which the entire human somatic structure is the instrument, and the Life which is the Universe: "All things were made by him and without him was not anything made that was made. In him was life, and the life was the light of men." This unitary vision, subscribed to by all the great Medieval "men of knowledge" (who were precisely not those anonymous technologists whose thinking gave rise to the great inventions), was clearly founded, then, not upon any sensory-material unity of nature, but upon a spiritual unity.

Thus the Prime Matter of the alchemists is not in any sense matter as we know it; rather it is the seed or water of life, the unmediated Divine Presence, and in this sense the feminine element, even the Holy Spirit. "If God could become man," wrote Novalis, demonstrating the continuity of this way of thinking, "then He can also become stone, plant, animal, and element, and perhaps in this way there is a continuous redemption in Nature."[4] From this perspective of a hierarchy of aspects of *consciousness*, each one sacrificing itself to another, the shift from science to technology may be seen not only in terms of a movement from unity to multiplicity or spirit to matter, but also, as Schwaller de Lubicz indicated in an early text, as the degeneration of Love into utility.

This is again a loss of orientation for, hermetically, creation as well as the knowledge of it, which is but its conscious return and identity in its source, is Love. Pherecydes of Syros, for instance, by tradition a teacher of Pythagoras, taught that:

> Zeus, when about to create, changed himself into Love; for in composing the order of the world out of the contraries he brought it to concord and friendship, and in all things he set the seed of identity and the unity which pervades everything.[5]

Pherecydes is "Hermetic" because he was learned in the Prophecies of Ham and in the secret books of the Phoenicians, whose revelation is attributed to *Thoth* or *Hermes*, "the master," according to Horopollo, "of the heart and reason in all men." According to another text, Hermes or Thoth is "the great, the only God, the Soul of Becoming," and as such is the mediator through whom the world is brought into manifestation, the master of creation, of every aspect and level of the formal world.

Hermes in this sense is thus the Patron of all science and knowledge, the judge and equilibrator of all polarity and

relation. He is Hermes Trismegistus, Thrice Great, Master
of the Three Worlds, and to him was ascribed all knowledge in the ancient world. As Archetypal Man he was the
primordial culture-bringer, the instituter of all arts, crafts
and sciences. He is healer, master architect, founder of
agriculture, smelting and mining; his Temple was called
the "House of the Net," which may be taken to indicate
cosmology or the weaving of the world fabric or garment,
each knot of which represents a conjunction of life and
death, impulse and resistance, contraction and expansion.
From this point of view, Hermes-Thoth is one with Enoch,
Idris, Quetzalcoatl, Odin — leaders of Humanity in the
celestial world from which they guide and sustain terrestrial
manifestation.[6]

We may also note, in connection with the idea of Archetypal Humanity or Perfect Nature, that, being so closely
associated with ideas of cosmos and mediation, Hermes-
Thoth frequently invokes the idea of the Celestial Witness
or the Philosopher's Angel. This Witness or *Daimon*, il-
luminator of "the knowledge and mysteries of Creation,
the causes of Nature, and the origins and modalities of
things" is simultaneously, as Henry Corbin has shown,
"the one who gives birth and the one who is born."[7] "The
seeing through which I know Him is the same seeing
through which He knows me," wrote Meister Eckhart.
Similarly, "the Mind of Sovereignty" or the *Poimandres*,
meaning Shepherd or Witness, states in the treatise of that
name in the *Corpus Hermeticum*: "I know what you wish,
for indeed I am with you everywhere; keep in mind all that
you desire to learn and I will teach you. . . . Learn my
meaning . . . by looking at what you yourself have in
you."[8]

Besides the *Corpus Hermeticum,* that collection of

Hellenistic "gnostic" texts purporting to be a transmission from Egypt and to represent a *summa* of Egyptian cosmology,* a good indication of Hermetic teaching is given by Orphic-Pythagorean and Platonic literature, Egyptian mythology, the *Enneads* of Plotinus and certain gnostic and alchemical texts such as the *Megale Apophasis*[9] and those attributed to Pseudo-Demokritus, Zosimos, Kleopatra, Maria the Jewess and Olympiodorus.[10] A study of these texts reveals, in the first place, that the cosmos is a unity of consciousness and life:

> "The Kosmos is an instrument of God's will, and it was made by Him to this end, that, having received from God the seeds of all things that belong to it, and keeping these seeds within itself, it might bring all things into actual existence. The Kosmos produces life in all things by its movement; and decomposing them, it renews the things that have been decomposed; for, like a good husbandman, it gives them renewal by sowing seed. There is nothing in which the Kosmos does not generate life; and it is both the place in which life is contained and the maker of life."
>
> (*Corpus Hermeticum* IX)

Again, in Book XIII Hermes says that the cosmos "is one mass of life, and there is not anything in the Kosmos that is not alive." However, the cosmos is not itself the source of life. The source of life is the Good, which is "full of immortal life."

Accordingly, in Plato's *Timaeus,* the Creator or Demiurge sought to make the universe a single, visible, living being — an organism — with body, soul and intelligence.

---

* It is not impossible in fact that the *Corpus Hermeticum* represents another initiatic cultural venture of the Ptolemies, comparable to their Septuagint translation of the Old Testament and their institution of the Mysteries of Isis and Serapis.

This he did in the model of the most completely perfect synthesis and seed of all intelligible things: "the perfect living creature." And the latter, Proclus tells us in his *Commentaries on the Timaeus*,[11] is none other than the first-begotten threefold archetypal Orphic Man of Light called *Phanes* (Shining), *Erikepaios* (Power, male) and *Metis* (Wisdom, female). In the words of the Orphic Hymn:

> Erikepaios, seed unforgettable, attended by many rites, ineffable, hidden, brilliant scion, whose motion is whirring, you scattered the dark mist that lay before your eyes, and, flapping your wings, you whirled about, and throughout this world you brought pure light.[12]

This Phanes, also called Eros and Dionysius is, in the myth, born of the Cosmic Egg formed by the polarization or doubling, of *Chronos,* the Principle of Principles, into *Aether* (a male principle of Limitation or Distinction) and *Chaos* (a female principle of Unlimitedness).[13] Now, since mutual love, or affinity, draws Male and Female into One, it is clear that the original division—scission or severance—is, at the same time, the original union. "Great is the mystery of marriage," says the gnostic *Gospel of Philip* "for without it the world would not have existed."[14] Just so, in Pherecydes' cosmology, too, there is a Primal Triad—*Chronos, Zas, Chthonie*—and the world arises out of the "wedding" of Zas and Chthonie.[15] Socrates, in the *Philebus,* puts it thus:

> There is a gift of the gods—so at least it seems evident to me—which they let fall from their abode, and it was through Prometheus, or one like him, that it reached mankind, together with a fire exceeding bright. The men of old, who were better than ourselves and dwelt nearer the gods, passed on this gift in the form of a saying. All things, so it ran, that are ever said to be consist of a one

and a many, and have in their nature a conjunction of limit and unlimitedness.[16]

For this reason Plato describes the Soul as formed out of the Same and the Different, two principles which will become the Fire and Water, Sulphur and Mercury of Medieval alchemy. These primordial complements exist in perpetual struggle but find their fulfillment in union or matrimony, as symbolized by the interpenetrating triangles of the Hexagram. This we may take to assert the mutual and radical interdependence of the Unity of Consciousness and the Multiplicity of Existence, of Transcendence and Immanence, of the Divine and its Presence. Phanes, then, this Egg or Seed and perfect conjunction — "original Man in the Fiat Lux" — is Light and Life, illuminating, animating all things in itself. Thus Phanes, Seed of seeds — and thereby the seed of all things, in their essence as in their unfolding — is constituted of polarity and conjunction. "What is not Life that really *is*?" wrote Coleridge.[17] In the identity of the two counterpowers, which for Coleridge were "light" and "gravitation," life subsisted; in their reconciliation it at once died and was born again into a new form.

The Hermetic universe, then, is alive and is a unity, life and unity arising out of conjunction or an identity of complements. A manuscript of the *Goldmaking* of Kleopatra expresses this idea to perfection: a serpent with its tail in its mouth encloses the motto *En to Pan,* One the All. Another text states: "One is the All, and thanks to it the All, and by it the All, and if the All did not contain the All, the All would be nothing."[18] The circle is closed. The universe is a uni-verse; there is nothing else: it is one-only, nonexteriorized and everything is connected to everything else. The *Corpus Hermeticum* (XVI) says: "If any one attempts to separate all things from the One, taking the term all things to signify a mere plurality of things, and not a whole made up of things, he will sever the All from the One, and will thereby bring to naught the All." Likewise, Ostanes, in the earliest alchemical formula, affirms: "Nature rejoices in Nature, Nature triumphs over Nature, Nature dominates Nature."[19]

What is involved here is obviously not a theory, nor any kind of reductionist, monist speculation, but an experience — the experience of a state of consciousness in which the opposition between subject and object, inside and outside, observer and observed is transcended to reveal the spiritual unity and creative interdependence of humanity and the cosmos. Thus the Hermetic universe, the Hermetic work, and the human subject are in certain respects one and the same. "Everything is the product of one universal creative effort," wrote Paracelsus, "the Macrocosm and man (the Microcosm) are one. They are one constellation, one influence, one breath, one harmony, one time, one metal, one fruit."[20] As Hermes teaches in the *Asclepius*, "Man is all things; man is everywhere." Such is the teaching which, emerging in the fifteenth century, was to inspire the Renaissance:

> None of the gods of heaven will ever quit heaven, and pass its boundary, and come down to earth; but man ascends even to heaven, and measures it; and what is more than all beside, he mounts to heaven without quitting the earth; to so vast a distance can he put forth his power. We must not shrink then from saying that a man on earth is a mortal god, and that a god in heaven is an immortal man.
>
> *(Corpus Hermeticum X)*

Thereby we return to the great postulate: the first, the seed of all, was "Man." To realize this was and is the great mystery, the Christian Mystery, foretold by "Pagan"

Hermeticism and then practiced by Christian Hermeticism. To know it is to be saved. It is knowledge, the beginning of science, but to know in this way is to be born again: begotten by the will of God, through a seed which is the true God, conceived in silence, in a womb which is wisdom. Reborn in this way, as in the famous Hermetic "Treatise Concerning Rebirth" (*Corpus Hermeticum* XIII), one comes to perceive "not with bodily eyesight, but by the working of mind," and a new science of revelation becomes possible:

> Father, now that I see in mind, I see myself to be the All. I am in heaven and on earth, in water and in air; I am in beasts and plants; I am a babe in the womb, and one that is not yet conceived, and one that has been born; I am present everywhere.

If one would know God, one must become like God, for only like may know like. But becoming like God in order to know God, one comes to know like God. Indeed, in a sense, the knowing with which one comes to know God is the knowing with which He knows. And thus as all things are in God, so they must also become in man; and since they are not in God as in a place, or space, corporeally, but rather invisibly, beyond space and time, the human being must also withdraw from space and time, matter and motion; and outside space and time consciousness is all. There are no continents in mind, nor elephants, nor any distance or time between galaxies or aeons. With each thought, as the *Corpus Hermeticum* (XI) says, we *are* there. There is only the present.

This is the teaching:

> If then you do not make yourself equal to God, you cannot apprehend God; for like is known by like. Leap clear of all

that is corporeal, and make yourself grow to a like expanse
with that greatness which is beyond all measure; rise above
all time, and become eternal; then you will apprehend
God. Think that for you too nothing is impossible; deem
that you too are immortal, and that you are able to grasp
all things in your thought, to know every craft and every
science; find your home in the haunts of every living
creature; make yourself higher than all heights, and lower
than all depths; bring together in yourself all opposites of
quality, heat and cold, dryness and fluidity; think that you
are everywhere at once, on land, at sea, in heaven; think
that you are not yet begotten, that you are in the womb,
that you are young, that you are old, that you have died,
that you are in the world beyond the grave; grasp in your
thought all this at once, all times and places, all substances
and qualities and magnitudes together; then you can apprehend God. But if you shut up your soul in your body,
and abase yourself, and say, "I know nothing, I can do
nothing, I am afraid of earth and sea, I cannot mount to
heaven: I know not what I was, nor what I shall be"; then,
what have you to do with God? Your thought can grasp
nothing beautiful and good, if you cleave to the body, and
are evil.

To realize this vision requires a radical transformation of
consciousness or perception, a change in the way in which
we know and perceive, "for all things which the eye can see
are mere phantoms and unsubstantial outlines; but the
things which the eye cannot see are the realities. . . ." (*Corpus Hermeticum* VI)

Here once again there is great unanimity in the tradition.
Plato in his *Timaeus*, for instance, constantly refers to the
distinction between knowledge (*episteme*) and opinion
(*doxa*), the one apprehensible by "intelligence with the aid
of reasoning," the other "the object of opinion and irra-

tional sensation"; and Paracelsus, too, most forcefully contrasts knowledge (*wissen und erkantnuss*) which is experience (*Erfahrung*) with pseudo-knowledge or *logica*, which is a figment of the rational mind, "a foreign doctrine." This, he says, is "the leaven of the Pharisees who move about in the schools, who break the power of nature and follow neither Christ nor the natural light."[21] These Pharisees are "the dead who bury the dead; there is no life in what they do, for there is no light for them in which they can learn anything."

The *Corpus Hermeticum* (X) puts it this way:

> Then only will you see it, when you cannot speak of it; for the knowledge of it is deep silence, and suppression of all the senses. . . . Knowledge differs greatly from sense-perception. Sense-perception takes place when that which is material has the mastery; and it uses the body as its organ, for it cannot exist apart from the body. But knowledge is incorporeal; the organ which it uses is the mind itself.

What is necessarily implied—leaving aside for the moment the question as to whether there has been an evolution or rearrangement of the relations constitutive of consciousness—is a schooling of the senses, a cleansing of "the doors of perception," so that these, instead of being "stuffed up with the gross mass of matter" and "crammed with loathly pleasures," may become once more *active* organs of true vision. This once achieved, one may "see with the heart him whose will it is that with the heart alone he should be seen." This is what later students will term *imaginatio vera*: True Imagination, the Star in Man.

Sensory phenomena appear to exist independently of us in time and space, and yet the world lives only because it speaks to us in a language we can understand, its meaning becoming alive for us to the extent that we assimilate it in experience. If we were aware (awake) and could direct our habitual responses—could see through our eyes rather than with them (realizing that an eye never saw anything)—we might realize that in each moment of perception it is we who bring meaning to bear upon the world; and that at the level from which meaning derives, of which our intuition of meaning is a recollection, there is no inside and outside but simply one world of Archetypal Imagining, outside time, where each thing *is,* without any comparison. Perception is thus more truly a remembering and we stand towards the spiritual world as towards a forgotten actuality. Indeed, it is simply our sensory apparatus that divides the world into inside and outside, giving to time and space an outerness they do not have.

However, we need not infer from this that the sensory function itself is in any way unnecessary or prone to error. On the contrary, it is the source of knowledge. "The knowledge of man comes from the greater world, not from himself," states Paracelsus, adding paradoxically that these two (the greater world and man) are "one thing and not two."

What he means becomes clear when we realize that by knowledge he means experience, which he contrasts with "experiment," the latter being "accidental." For instance, experiment may teach us the "fact" that a certain herb— Scammonea—purges or rather that there is a virtue or knowledge in the Scammonea which teaches it how to purge, just as there is a knowledge in the pear tree which teaches it how to grow pears. Objective observation, "experiment," apprises us of this fact, but truly experienced knowledge is union with the knowledge in the Scammonea: "When you overhear from the Scammonea the knowledge which it possesses, it will be in you just as it is in the Scammonea and you have acquired the experience as well as the knowledge."

Knowledge, then, from this point of view, is the nonobjectified understanding of the way in which, as Walter Pagel puts it, "any particular natural object fulfills itself and thereby attains perfection—its inborn and sure instinctive 'knowledge.' " In other words: "that 'knowledge' is 'correct' which enables an object to realize its specific aims."[22]

We may now go further and compare these two kinds of knowing with two ways of "perceiving." In the first, which is ordinary sense-perception, the object perceived is immediately transformed or abstracted into a representation, while in the second the perception is not abstracted or transformed but rather, as it were, allowed to germinate in the soul. As Rudolf Steiner notes, we may compare perception here to a grain of corn or wheat which may either be eaten or be planted in the soul. He remarks: "Whenever a seed of corn is processed for the purposes of nutrition, it is lifted out of the developmental pattern which is proper to it, and which ends in the formation of a new plant; but so also is a representation, whenever it is applied by the mind in producing a mental copy of a sense-perception, diverted from its proper teleological pattern."[23]

To plant a perception in the soul is to allow it to complete itself, to reveal its "knowledge," whereas to fix it in a representation, a "picture," is to reduce it to mental fodder. Rather than catching the bird in flight and flying with it, we shoot it down and so kill it; hence we live with dead thoughts, not living ones. True sense-perception, therefore, not only works to recall the inner sense to its spiritual archetype but also permits the exaltation of phenomena through individualized self-knowledge, now revealed to be none other than world knowledge under an individualized aspect. "True imagination," writes Maurice Aniane, "actually 'sees' the 'subtle' processes of nature and their angelic prototypes. It is the capacity to reproduce in oneself the cosmogenic unfolding, the permanent creation of the world in the sense in which all creation, finally, is only a Divine Imagination."[24]

This philosophy of perception is at once a philosophy of symbols, a symbolism or "symbolic method," and a phenomenalism. For all phenomena are symbols or symbolic from this point of view. They are the necessary representations or bearers of the knowledge they contain or embody—the knowledge being that which makes them what they are, the principle according to which they function. Thus each thing in nature—each bird, tree and flower—is, as it were, a question containing its own potential answer, meaning and explanation. All phenomena—light, color, sound—and all natural processes—germination, growth, digestion, fermentation—contain the power to evoke, in the prepared observer, if he does not shoot them down, the true response that is their meaning. This Hermetic doctrine of the reciprocity of man and world is well represented by Goethe when he writes: "Man knows himself only insofar as he knows the world, becoming aware of it only within himself, and of himself only within it. Each new subject, well observed, opens up within us a new organ of thought."[25] Accordingly, in this philosophy lies the foundation of a true science of phenomena, a science of the commonplace, essentially dispensing with all instrumentation and relying on consciousness alone—for consciousness here is everything. Goethe says: "The best of all would be to realize that every fact is already theory. The blue of the sky shows us the principles of color. We need not look for anything behind phenomena: they themselves are the doctrine."[26] Hermetic science is therefore able to understand such phenomena as life, light, space, time, matter (which our science precisely cannot fathom), because it is able to experience phenomena as such, that is to say, as God Himself knows them.

In other words—and this is most important—we must go beyond the idea of a single, unique act of creation and assume as well a "creative state" of continuous or recurrent creation, metaphysical in nature, outside space and time. From this point of view creation is continuously or recurrently unfolding, and consciousness may always "know" its states by virtue of the principle whereby "the One is the All." Hermetically, that is, to "know" a god is to penetrate to a specific creative phase or relationship. As Ortolanus says, "Our Stone is made in the same way that the world is created."[27] Consequently, the world is not continuous as our senses present it to us, but there are moments of eternity, gaps or openings in perception, which our senses conceal from us. Indeed, for the Hermeticist, it is just by means of these "gaps" that causality—out of time—is effected by means of the gods who are themselves the "causes." Causality is therefore vertical, for in the realm of phenomena—the horizontal plane—there are only connections without cause.

It follows from this, since "the path up and down is one and the same" as Heraclitus said,[28] that continuous creation is, and contains, the mystery of Resurrection. Creation is theophany; theophany is theosis: "I was a hidden treasure, I yearned to be known. That is why I produced creatures, in order to be known by them."[29]

It is not difficult, then, to see why Hermetic alchemy has been called "the science of the symbol" in contrast to modern science, which is rather "the science of representation." For if knowledge of creation depends upon the ascent of the soul then, as Corbin says, imagination and theophany—the way up and the way down—are but other terms for what is called in Islamic esotericism *ta'wil*, that spiritual exegesis whereby things, natural objects as well as scriptural meanings, are "led back" from their outerness, their letter, to their innerness or spirit—a process that can take place only in the soul. Thus *ta'wil* becomes a word for the "continuous ascent of the soul" through the world hieroglyphically conceived as made of symbols and images; all phenomena from this perspective, then, are twofold, ineffable *coincidentiae oppositorum*, conjunctions of inner realities and outer facts, visible and invisible worlds, all of which implies an irreducible polarity, bi-dimensionality or reflexivity of being itself, and so of consciousness and life.[30]

"All things are but two," states the *Corpus Hermeticum* (XIV), "that which is made and that which makes. And the one cannot be separated from the other; the Maker cannot exist apart from the thing made, nor the thing made, apart from the Maker. Each of them is just that and nothing else; and so the one can no more be parted from the other than it can be parted from itself." So, too, male and female, heavenly and earthly. "When you make the two one," Jesus said, in the gnostic *Gospel of Thomas*, "you will become the sons of man, and when you say, 'Mountain, move away,' it will move away."[31] A Greek alchemical text makes all this a little clearer: "One becomes Two; Two becomes Three; and by means of the Third the Fourth realizes Unity. Thus the Two no longer form but One."[32] From the Hermetic point of view, this is the King, the perfect union of Creator and Creature, spirit and Soul, Sun and Moon, the Perfect Man.

Here, then, is the true end of Hermetic Science—to give birth to a Son of God, in contradistinction to contemporary science whose only end is its own methodology. This is the tradition to which *Nature Word* belongs. Indeed, *Nature Word* is a remarkably concise, clear exposition of the fundamental ideas of this science. Necessarily, it is difficult. It is not, however, in any sense "archeological" or scholarly. It is rather absolutely contemporary and original for, though the knowledge may be one and unchanging, people and times change, and the knowledge must each time be won anew, because this knowledge is active and attainable only through profound personal experience, suffering and sacrifice. This is to say that although a study of great spiritual works of the past helps—indeed, is one of the two great "aids" in the Work, the other being the study of Nature—true Hermetic knowledge is finally achieved only through deep inward realization and effort. Thus each student of the Hermetic speaks in his own voice, from his own experience. Nature and Scripture may have been his guides, but his only justification for speaking is that he knows.

The perenniality of the Hermetic tradition having been affirmed, something must be said, however briefly, of its history, or evolution, as this is not unconnected to our present situation which is, after all, what Schwaller de Lubicz is addressing.

There are, of course, several histories, but the most appropriate to relate is that which began in Egypt, in a hierarchical, caste society. Herein all activity derived from the Temple, receiving from it its form and substance. The arts, crafts and sciences were ritualized, initiatic embodiments of the metaphysical and theological knowledge realized by the priestcraft. Under this sacerdotal guidance, Egypt achieved a unique level of perfection in which all functions and languages — those of myth, theology, hieroglyph, and geometry, for instance — were interconnected. At the shift of the World Age at the time of Christ, however, these connections were broken, the wisdom of Egypt was cast haphazardly into the creative ferment of the moment, and Greco-Roman alchemy, at once craft, philosophy and religion, was born.

The earliest "alchemical" texts available to us (such as the Leyden Papyrus and the Holm Papyrus) derive from this period and contain only recipes, *aides memoires* for the craftsman. However, appearing almost simultaneously with these are other texts, more Neo-Platonic, Neo-Pythagorean, and gnostic in character, in which the metaphysical principles are more openly stated with a view to their realization. That is, these texts are not works of philosophy, so much as they are manuals of "inner work" and self-initiation and hark back, as Jack Lindsay says, to ancient unity of craft-process and metaphysical principle. But the period — that of the political foundation of Christianity — was not propitious for freedom of individual thought and research and, as this was progressively diminished, alchemical, philosophical and hermetic texts and thinking moved eastwards, through Syria, into Persia. On the way, in an act of cultural transmission which has been compared by Henry Corbin to the transmission of Mahayana Buddhism from Sanskrit into Chinese, a great accumulated body of literature was translated. This transfer was providential, for it meant that the fully flowering fruit of Hellenistic science and philosophy lay ready to be received by Islam with the result that, within 150 years of its founding, Islamic alchemy had reached its height with Jabir, whose immense oeuvre of over three thousand

34

treatises, though having some laboratory usefulness, is predominantly psycho-spiritual in intent.

Jabir is particularly interesting for us in the context of *Nature Word* because of his use of the so-called *Emerald Tablet* in his *Second Book of the Element of the Foundation*, discovered by E.J. Holmyard in 1923. Until Holmyard's discovery, this epitome of alchemical philosophy was known only in medieval Latin versions. More recently, however, another Arabic version has been found, ascribed to Appolonius of Tyana.[33] In other words, the *Tabula Smaragdina* also came, according to tradition, probably from Egypt via Greece and Persia, as we would expect.

This famous text, to which Schwaller de Lubicz refers on a number of occasions and upon which *Nature Word* in some sense constitutes a commentary, is quoted here in full as a useful reference for the reader:

> In truth, certainly and without doubt, whatever is below is like that which is above, and whatever is above is like that which is below, to accomplish the miracles of one thing.
>
> Just as all things proceed from One alone by meditation on One alone, so also they are born from this one thing by adaptation.
>
> Its father is the sun and its mother is the moon. The wind has borne it in its body. Its nurse is the earth.
>
> It is the father of every miraculous work in the whole world.
>
> Its power is perfect if it is converted into earth.
>
> Separate the earth from the fire and the subtle from the gross, softly and with great prudence.
>
> It rises from earth to heaven and comes down again from heaven to earth, and thus acquires the power of the realities above and the realities below. In this way you will acquire the glory of the whole world, and all darkness will leave you.

35

This is the power of all powers, for it conquers everything subtle and penetrates everything solid.

Thus the little world is created according to the prototype of the great world.

From this and in this way, marvellous applications are made.

For this reason I am called Hermes Trismegistus, for I possess the three parts of wisdom of the whole world.

Perfect is what I have said of the work of the sun.[34]

From Islam, hermetic alchemy travelled to the Medieval West, *A Testament of Alchemy* of Morienus,[35] the first work to be translated, arriving in 1144. Other translations followed and soon original works began to be written in Latin, with Artephius, Albertus Magnus, Thomas Aquinas, Roger Bacon, Raymond Lull, Arnald of Villanova and Nicholas Flamel all continuing the tradition of bringing that which is imperfect into perfection. However, we may note that, apart from such a work as John Scotus Eriugena's *On the Division of Nature*,[36] alchemy in the West lacked any real metaphysical foundation except as embodied in its own techniques and in Scripture. Even so, mention must be made of the School of Chartres, which in its own way — through its Platonized hermeticism — laid the ground for the Renaissance and the explosive influence of Marsilio Ficino's translations. These, beginning with the *Corpus Hermeticum* in 1463 and thereafter including translations of Plato, Plotinus, Iamblichus, Porphyry, Proclus and the Chaldean Oracles, enabled Hermeticism to flower once more as "Renaissance Hermeticism" in the life and work of, for instance, Paracelsus, Bruno, the Rosicrucian Brotherhood, Van Helmont, Basil Valentine and Jacob Boehme.

From the point of view of the history of the Hermetic

tradition, however, what is interesting is that with the Renaissance alchemy and related hermetic sciences emerged from their position of occultation into the open air of history and actively sought to gain the ascendancy in the emerging scientific age. That is to say, the hermeticist turned "outward," not only in the sense of becoming more "engaged" socially, but also in that he turned his attention more consciously to "nature."

In the final analysis the sudden availability of texts, of course, is more a symptom than a cause of that revolutionary moment, or transformation of consciousness which we call the Renaissance, for what the Renaissance represents may in some sense be said to have matured slowly throughout the entire historical course of what the great Quaker Rufus Jones called "Spiritual Religion."[37] By this he meant that invisible Church founded by St. John (but taught also by St. Paul), whose basis is:

> That which is born of flesh is flesh and that which is born of spirit is spirit. Marvel not that I said unto thee, Ye must be born again. The wind bloweth where it listeth, and thou hearest the sound thereof, but canst not tell whence it cometh and whither it goeth: so is everyone that is born of the Spirit.
>
> (John 3:6–8)

These seeds—revolutionary then as now—germinated slowly, only gradually giving rise to the consciousness of a human spiritual unity, a Cosmic Humanity, united in the "inner light" with God and with all beings—a Spiritual Being in whom all participated. Its task was to create a New Jerusalem, a spiritual city without walls, an invisible Temple whose altar was the human heart and whose name was the Universe. Here then is another history, or another level of history, and one which connects to the process—

foreshadowed perhaps by Plato—that led at once to the misplaced rationality and to the concretization of individual consciousness characteristic of our present situation.

The historical course of this tendency or impulse may be traced from Plato and Plotinus and from John and Paul, passing by groups of gnostics and other "heretics," through Saint Gregory of Nyssa and Dionysius the Areopagite, into the Medieval West where it gave birth once again, not only to that great movement of mystics such as Eckhart, Suso, Tauler, Ruysbroek, Nicholas of Cusa, the Friends of God, and the Brethren of the Common Life, but also to the "heresies" of the Cathars and the Waldenses. Then, with the Renaissance proper, this current of mystical spirituality, within which had been forming the new being ("man") that humanity was to become, merged with the now readily available Hermetic and Platonic teachings. Exoterically, perhaps, the result was the Reformation; esoterically, it was the renewal, the interiorization of the ancient view of the universe as a sacred, initiatic Temple—a Temple transformed and reborn through the saving work of Christ.

In this spirit *The Chemical Wedding of Christian Rosenkreutz*[38] begins on an "evening before Easter-day" and ends, the wedding consummated—Sun and Moon, Spirit and Soul perfectly united—with the formation of the Order of the Golden Stone and with the presentation of a golden medal, bearing on the one side the inscription *"Art is the Servant of Nature"* and on the other *"Nature is the Daughter of Time."* Knowledge must follow nature, imitate her in her mode of operation according to the adage of the alchemists, listen to her needs, attend her will. But nature, the world of becoming, is herself but an offspring, a moment of time, the finite fruit of an infinite evolutive faculty. Within nature there is no time: nature *is* time, time *is* nature, they are an inseparable, identical process. Having learned this, the new Knights are given their articles, enjoining them to ascribe their order "only to God and his hand-maid Nature," to overcome their lower natures, and to place themselves fully at the service of humanity for the sake, and in the reality, of the Spirit. Finally, they all sign their names, Christian Rosenkreutz appending to his the motto *Summa scientia nihil scire*, "the height of knowledge is to know nothing."

Outwardly, of course, the story of the origins of modern science is extremely complex and probably not to be rationally understood. Suffice it to say that Hermetic, Platonic and Rosicrucian influences were continuously at play in the formation of the new scientific attitude; that Ficino, Bruno, Paracelsus, Dee, Fludd, Van Helmont and other representatives of the tradition worked openly to create a "new world," a new science, art and religion—a new society—and that the old order recoiled, persecuting the "new men" as fanatics, madmen and heretics, so that materialism and mechanism won the day. It must be added, however, and this is critical, that in addition to being aweful in its newness what was actually at stake in the struggle was much more complex: a new state of *consciousness*. For what the Renaissance, in its mystics and hermeticists, modestly proclaimed was the need for (and hence possibility of) a new "initiation," a new and powerful science of nature based upon a transformation of consciousness, a new way of knowing. Something that had previously been the exclusive province of the Saint, monk or hermit was now taught to be the birthright of every human being, attainable with the aid of God alone by virtue of the "inner light" of human consciousness. Rufus Jones writes:

One comes back from a study of the Quaker literature of the seventeenth century with the profound impression that these Children of the Light did actually have a fresh revelation of God. The most remarkable thing about the movement is not that its leaders founded a new state, or worked out a new and, I think, an extraordinarily happy form of religious organization, or discovered a new principle of social fellowship, or inaugurated a new type of human service; it is, rather, that they came into a new experience of the present reality and the living presence of God. They passed from a religion based upon the accumulated deposit of other men's faith, and on the authority of books and creeds, to a religion based on their own vision of God, and tested by their own experience of His transforming power.[39]

No wonder, then, that the Church chose materialism instead when the alternative so clearly threatened organized religion. The choice was between the death of the Church as a human artifact and the death of God. The Church, naturally, chose the latter. However, one must not scoff. There are no "sides" in the gestating continuum of history. History is all of a piece, complete in itself, and we ought perhaps always to give the benefit of the doubt to providence, of which human action, with its tragedies and uncertainties — its freedom — is the embodiment. That is to say, that only now might we be truly able to realize the promise foreseen in the Renaissance.

In any event, after the first pulsation, the impulse died away, went underground, only to return with renewed vigor and a new form, as Romanticism or the "romantic" path to higher knowledge. From this point of view Goethe, Coleridge, Blake, Keats, Novalis, Lamartine, de Nerval — and even the philosophers Fichte, Schelling, von Baader and Hegel — are all manifestations of the "symbolic method," which is Hermeticism. The Romantics too, like their predecessors, tried to proclaim a new science of the spirit. But the impetus towards materialism was set and not yet ready to be transformed. Theirs was therefore a prophetic mission, one perhaps only able to come to fruition in our own time, when, in the words of Owen Barfield, referring to Rudolf Steiner, "Romanticism comes of Age." He may as well have said, "The Renaissance comes of Age."

Nature Word is of this lineage, a third call, renewing the summons to a science of the spirit first sounded by Paracelsus and Ficino, the original Romantics. Perhaps now, finally, the stage is set. Certainly philosophers such as Nietzsche, Bergson, Whitehead, Heidegger, Gadamer, and Ricoeur have begun to dismantle the fortress of Cartesian consciousness and to replace it with a consciousness open to the mystery of revelation and the process of existence, which is itself consciousness, and in which human beings participate by the mediation of signs, the surrender to which discloses truth. In science, too, physicists such as Einstein, Heisenberg, de Broglie, von Weizsacker and Bohm, logicians such as G. Spencer Brown and the whole emerging paradigm of self-organization in biology and the origin of life, have brought contemporary thinking uncannily close to the Hermetic. The time, then, is ripe to consider such a work as *Nature Word*.

The issue is quite clear. Everyone agrees about the need to learn to think in a new way. But how is this to be achieved? For Heidegger, philosophy has become "thinking otherwise" but, tragically, "the greatness of what must be thought remains too great" and no thinker appears great enough "to bring thought before its proper business immediately and in resolute form." His conclusion is: "Only a god can save us now."[40]

41

Gregory Bateson, too, realized the life-and-death necessity of learning to think in a new way; but when it came to making that way of thinking habitual he was pessimistic about the possibility. Other instances could be cited to show that modern science and thinking has reached a limit—the limit of a sense-based rationality—and that, in the face of this limitation it is not sure how to proceed. Meanwhile, "things fall apart and the center cannot hold."

Schwaller de Lubicz is unhesitating. A leap, a reversal is necessary. For science and knowledge to be reborn it must first die. The consequences of such a position, the implications of turning thought against itself in this way, are enormous—indeed, they are total. However, he may just be right, and certainly what he proposes is a positive alternative. Moreover, it is on the side of Life; on the side of Truth, Beauty and Goodness; on the side of Freedom, Humanity and Responsibility. Given today's state of affairs, so well known that it need not be itemized, we would do well to study his work closely.

CHRISTOPHER BAMFORD
1981

NOTES

1. Werner Foerster, *Gnosis: A Selection of Gnostic Texts*, vol. 1, *Patristic Evidence*, ed. R. McL. Wilson (Oxford: Oxford University Press, 1972), p. 197.

2. Martin Heidegger, *The Question Concerning Technology and Other Essays*, trans. William Lovitt (New York: Harper & Row, Publishers, 1977), p. 115.

3. Owen Barfield, *What Coleridge Thought* (Middletown, Conn.: Wesleyan University Press, 1971), pp. 20, 25.

4. Novalis, *Hymns to the Night and Other Selected Writings*, trans. Charles E. Passage, The Library of Liberal Arts (New York: Bobbs-Merrill Company, 1960), p. 72.

5. Simone Weil, *On Science, Necessity, and the Love of God*, comp., ed., and trans. Richard Rees (London: Oxford University Press, 1968), p. 139.

6. See G.R.S. Mead, *Thrice Greatest Hermes: Studies in Hellenistic Theosophy and Gnosis*, 3 vols. (London: John M. Watkins, 1964), 1:36–55.

   René Guénon, "Hermes," *The Sword of Gnosis*, ed. Jacob Needleman (Baltimore: Penguin Books, 1974), pp. 370–375.

   Seyyed Hossein Nasr, *Islamic Studies, Essays on law and society, the sciences, and philosophy and Sufism* (Beirut: Libraire du Liban, 1967) pp. 63–89.

7. See Henry Corbin, *The Man of Light in Iranian Sufism*, trans. Nancy Pearson (Boulder: Shambhala, 1978).

8. This and the following quotes from the *Corpus Hermeticum* are from Walter Scott, *Hermetica*, 4 vols. (Oxford: Oxford University Press, 1924–1936).

9. Foerster, *Gnosis*, pp. 251–260.

10. See Jack Lindsay, *The Origins of Alchemy in Graeco-Roman Egypt* (London: Frederick Muller Ltd., 1970).

11. Thomas Taylor, trans., *The Commentaries of Proclus on the Timaeus of Plato*, 2nd ed., printed for and sold by the author (London: 1820), p. 272.

12. Apostolos N. Athanassakis, trans., *The Orphic Hymns*, Society of Biblical Literature, Graeco-Roman Series 4 (Missoula, Mont.: Scholars Press, 1977), p. 11.

13. For Orphic cosmology see W.K.C. Guthrie, *Orpheus and Greek Religion* (New York: W.W. Norton, 1966).

14. Wesley W. Isenberg, trans., "The Gospel of Philip," *The Nag Hammadi Library*, ed. James M. Robinson (San Francisco: Harper & Row, Publishers, 1977), p. 139.

15. G.S. Kirk and J.E. Raven, *The Presocratic Philosophers* (Cambridge: Cambridge University Press, 1957), pp. 48–71.

16. R. Hackforth, trans., "Philebus," *The Collected Dialogues of Plato*, eds. Edith Hamilton and Huntington Cairns, Bollingen Series LXXI (Princeton: Princeton University Press, 1961), p. 1092.

17. Barfield, *What Coleridge Thought*, p. 49.

18. J. Evola, *La Tradition Hermétique* (Paris: Éditions Traditionnelles, 1975), p. 32.

19. Lindsay, *Origins of Alchemy*, p. 33.

20. Franz Hartmann, *The Life of Paracelsus and the Substance of his Teachings*, 2nd ed., rev. and enl. (London: Keegan Paul, Trench, Trübner & Co. Ltd., n.d.), p. 47.

21. Walter Pagel, *Paracelsus, An Introduction to Philosophical Medicine in the Era of the Renaissance* (Basel: S. Karger AG, 1958), pp. 56, 58.

44

22. Ibid., p. 60.

23. Rudolf Steiner, *The Case for Anthroposophy*, comp. and trans. Owen Barfield (London: Rudolf Steiner Press, 1970), p. 37.

24. Maurice Aniane, "Notes on Alchemy, the Cosmological 'Yoga' of Medieval Christianity," *Material for Thought*, Spring 1976, p. 78.

25. Bertha Mueller, trans., *Goethe's Botanical Writings* (Honolulu: University of Hawaii Press, 1952), p. 235.

26. From *The Principles of Natural Science*, as quoted in *The Wisdom of Goethe*, comp. Emil Ludwig, trans. F. Melian Stawell and Nora Purtscher-Wydenbruck (New York: Carlton House, n.d.), p. 89.

27. Evola, *La Tradition Hermétique*, p. 40, n. 1.

28. Kirk and Raven, *The Presocratic Philosophers*, p. 189.

29. A saying from a *Hadith Quidsi*, or "Sacred Tradition," attributed to the prophet Mohammed, in which God speaks through him in the first person.

30. Henry Corbin, *Avicenna and the Visionary Recital*, trans. Willard R. Trask, Bollingen Series LXVI (New York: Pantheon Books, 1960), pp. 28–35.

31. Thomas O. Lambdin, trans., "The Gospel of Thomas," *The Nag Hammadi Library*, p. 129.

32. Evola, *La Tradition Hermétique*, p. 51.

33. E.J. Holmyard, *Alchemy* (Harmondsworth, Middlesex: Penguin Books, 1957), pp. 81, 97–99.

34. Titus Burckhardt, *Alchemy: Science of the Cosmos, Science of the Soul*, trans. William Stoddart (Baltimore: Penguin Books, 1971), pp. 196–197.

35. Lee Stavenhagen, ed. and trans., *A Testament of Alchemy: Being the Revelations of Morienus to Khālid Ibn Yazīd* (Hanover, N.H.: Brandeis University Press, The University Press of New England, 1974).

36. John the Scot (Joannes Scotus Eriugena), *Periphyseon: On the Division of Nature*, ed. and trans. Myra L. Uhlfelder, The Library of Liberal Arts (Indianapolis: Bobbs-Merrill Company, 1976).

37. Rufus Jones, *Spiritual Reformers in the 16th and 17th Centuries* (Boston: Beacon Press, 1959), p. xi.

38. Arthur Edward Waite, *Real History of the Rosicrucians* (Blauvelt, N.Y.: Steinerbooks, 1977), pp. 99–196.

39. Rufus Jones, *The Radiant Life* (New York: The Macmillan Company, 1944), p. 138.

40. " 'Only a God Can Save Us Now': An Interview with Martin Heidegger," trans. David Schendler, *Graduate Faculty Research Journal* 6, no. 1 (Winter 1977), pp. 25, 27.

Introduction

‰————————————————————————‰

R.A. Schwaller de Lubicz
and *Nature Word*

THE WORK of R.A. Schwaller de Lubicz (1887–1961),
though widely known in his native France, has only in recent years been introduced to this country through the publication of *The Temple in Man* (1977) and *Symbol and the
Symbolic* (1978), both dealing with architecture, myth and
symbol, particularly in ancient Egypt. Hence Schwaller de
Lubicz is principally known to American readers as an in-
terpreter of Egyptian culture, yet his work in Egypt,
although occupying many of his mature years, should be
seen in the context of the entire spectrum of his work as
rather a verification, application and extension of his
primary activity as a philosopher.

At the age of fourteen, René Schwaller precociously but
earnestly posed the problem: "What is the origin of matter?"[1] This seminal question was to remain at the core of
his philosophical inquiry. Indeed, in his last book, *Le Roi de
la Théocratie Pharaonique*, he notes that "the essential preoccupation of thinking man has always been to know the
origin of matter and existence" and shows how the fundamental questions of the origin of matter and the end (*raison
d'être*) of human existence are the two faces or polar aspects
of the Hermetic vision, otherwise called "Sacred Science."

[1] Biographical data compiled from Isha Schwaller de Lubicz, *"Aor":
Sa vie — Son oeuvre* (Paris: La Colombe, 1963), and from conversations
with Lucie Lamy, Schwaller de Lubicz's stepdaughter and collaborator.

It was in pursuit of the outlines of this sacred science, that is, a science of sound metaphysical grounding whose method is in accord with nature's own procedures, that Schwaller began his philosophical quest, a quest that would eventually lead him, through many diverse studies, to formulate with ever increasing precision the nature of such a science.

In 1926 he attacked the problem of existence as posed by Descartes' proposition "I think, therefore I am." We know our existence, our "am-ness," Schwaller de Lubicz says, because we live it. What we do not know is what our form is nor what the forms are of the world that we perceive. With Schopenhauer and Nietzsche we may ask, "Do I pose the world or am I posed or projected by the world, by universal evolution?" Schwaller de Lubicz saw the question as revolving around the "I" which is either posed or projected, saying that the basic fact to be recognized is the very *self-identity* of the "I," the "I" before itself. This fact of self-identity led him to assert as ultimate metaphysical term the self-identity of the original cause, conceived as the One: Oneness before itself. The study of how this Oneness becomes multiplicity and evolution forms the framework of sacred science.

The unique position of mankind within universal becoming and the avenues of knowledge open to him within the context of sacred science were matters of passionate concern for Schwaller de Lubicz throughout his life. Although the basic position he formulated regarding these matters in the late 1920s changed very little during his lifetime, his means of expressing it evolved and matured considerably. Like an artist who nurtures a vocabulary of forms throughout a long life, he was able to turn his ideas in different lights, expose them to a variety of applications and, with entire

48

conviction, to live them. For this reason he was considered by many who knew him as not only a philosopher but an individual of profound inner development.

René Schwaller's principal interests as a boy in Strasbourg were painting and natural sciences. He performed chemical experiments in the laboratory of his father, a pharmacist, and as soon as, without drama, he could free himself from family life, he took up residence in Paris where he could study on his own. There he became the painting student of Matisse, with whom he remained for several years. Matisse's interest in the philosophy of Henri Bergson must have been communicated to his student, along with, one can imagine, the painter's sense that light and color emanating from a unique source is the permanent mystery through which the fleeting forms of things coagulate and dissolve. At the same time Schwaller continued to study physics and chemistry, as well as Pythagorean and Hermetic philosophy. Perhaps it was through the inspiration of these latter studies that he came to frequent, for two years, the Theosophical Society, where he was also invited to lecture. Soon after this he met the great Lithuanian poet and diplomat O.W. de Lubicz Milosz, with whom he was to collaborate in an attempt to persuade the Allies to sustain the Baltic States as an independent country.[2]

When the war broke out Schwaller became a chemist in

[2] In 1919, as a gesture of recognition for their friendship and work together, Milosz, who was head of the ancient Lubicz clan, made Schwaller a "brother" in an authentic chivalric ceremony, giving him the right to bear the name "Chevalier de Lubicz." The philosophic maturity of the younger man seems to have inspired and profoundly influenced the poet, whose "Cantique de la Connaissance" and other works reflect their dialogue.

the army but managed to continue his research. In 1917 he published his first book, *Étude sur les Nombres*, a study of Pythagorean principles, drawing especially on Theon of Smyrna. This was his first philosophic statement, based on the notion of Unity. Primary among the principles he enunciated here was the idea that to know the numbers in their successive "disengagement" from Unity is to know the universe and its unfoldment. Using the Pythagorean device of the tetraktys as a guide, he outlined the successive phases in the process of creation, whether it be on the level of the universe as a whole, or on that of an individual seed as it moves towards becoming fruit and new seed. He formulated the principles or universal functions governing each of these phases and defined the "Irreducible Unity" as the source of all creation. From its scission come successively the cycles of Polarization, Ideation and Formation; through these dynamics one cause produces all the "effects" which are the cosmos. Each of Schwaller de Lubicz's major works was to enrich and develop this theme of creation. His treatment of it in *Nature Word* consists of an important reformulation of the first four major functions as polarization (or scission), selection (or affinity), harmonization and individuation.

At the close of the war Schwaller de Lubicz's attention turned towards the social and moral issues of the time, and his influence among his peers was considerable. He founded a group in Paris called *Les Veilleurs*, composed mainly of artists and writers, seeking to re-establish meaningful values and goals after the moral turmoil of the war years.[3] Their

[3] Isha Schwaller de Lubicz outlines ("*Aor*," p. 16) the goals of *Les Veilleurs* as follows:

"— To combine the efforts of the citizens of all countries for the

journals, *L'Affranchi* and later *Le Veilleur*, stressed the importance of decentralization, individualism and meaningful work, and above all sought to stem the growing tide of the mechanization of all aspects of life. As the guiding force behind this movement and the formulator of its philosophical basis, Schwaller de Lubicz is remembered by those who knew him then as a dynamic and charismatic leader, although always quiet in demeanor. Thus *Les Veilleurs*, with unbounded enthusiasm (and dressed dashingly in clothing which required minimal machine sewing — simple tunics for the women and capes, boots and full blouses for the men), addressed themselves to such basic issues of the time as feminism, socialism, art, craftsmanship, the esoteric tradition, care of the earth and the hidden causes behind all things.

Never ceasing to absorb both philosophy (Hindu and Islamic metaphysics at this time) and modern physics (he followed closely the revolution in physics of the 1920s), Schwaller de Lubicz found it necessary after several years to withdraw from the active life of *Les Veilleurs* and to settle quietly in Switzerland, high above Saint-Moritz, with Isha ("Jeanne le Veilleur") and a group of student-friends. The fiery idealism of the days of *Les Veilleurs* now matured into

---

common defense of the principles of human rights, which are the unique and supreme safeguards of their independence and of their legitimate interests, and whose respect alone can assure a durable peace to the world.

" — To oppose with unrelenting energy the reawakening of all imperialism and the abuses which the great powers tend to commit to the detriment of smaller nations.

" — To intensify intellectual exchanges among peoples through the organization of conferences, the sending out of brochures and the publication of a periodical."

a sense of personal mission involving a profound interior research,[4] carried out within the context of a small community in which Schwaller de Lubicz and his wife were acknowledged as the educational and spiritual leaders. They established *Station Scientifique Suhalia* where a research center including laboratories for physics, chemistry, microphotography and the manufacture of homeopathic tinctures was set up, along with an astronomical observatory, a machine shop, workshops for woodworking, blacksmithing, printing, weaving, rugmaking and glassmaking and a theater. The researches in these diverse areas were all expressions of a single vital inquiry, the investigation of the fundamental harmonic laws of nature in their unfoldment from Unity. "Many artists and craftsmen," writes Isha Schwaller de Lubicz of this period, "came happily to Suhalia to participate in this research of perfection in work, guided and enlivened by numerous lectures."

Like a true "Renaissance man," Schwaller de Lubicz, motivated by the investigation into causes, was able to turn his hand to many tasks at Suhalia in an astonishing outflow of creative energy. With the goal of freeing France from dependence on petrol, he invented a motor to run on vegetable oil. He also designed, following principles of number

[4] Isah writes ("*Aor*," p. 20):
"Now the '*Mission*' consisted of showing contemporary man the definitive goal of his existence, and demonstrating to him the error of the mode of thinking which *deflects him from this goal*.
"The definitive goal is the identification of the *human Consciousness* with its immortal Entity. This means:
— the acquisition for terrestrial man of his immortality;
or again:
— the conscious reintegration of his spiritual being;
or again:
— the transcendence of the Human into the superhuman."

and proportion, a ship which proved to have remarkable properties of speed and balance in rough waters, did considerable work with plants and, in the manufacture of stained glass starting from sand, rediscovered the medieval "alchemical" method for achieving the brilliant red and blue found in the great cathedrals. Above all, he received the inspiration which coalesced his philosophic vision into a cohesive whole. In 1926 Schwaller de Lubicz published *L'Appel du Feu*, in which this inspiration or higher intelligence is personified as "Aor" (Hebrew for "intellectual light," and the name by which Schwaller de Lubicz himself was subsequently known) who speaks to the author, a form of presentation which he was to adopt again for *Nature Word*. *L'Appel du Feu* together with *La Doctrine*, published at Suhalia and distributed privately to his students, began to elaborate his philosophy of the evolution of consciousness. Their composition was the fruit of an intense concentration, described by Schwaller de Lubicz as a revelation:

> As for the doctrine which I wish to set forth for you, and in order to make my authoritative and personal words more authentic for you, here are the sources from which I draw this knowledge.
>
> First of all, I have inherited it, inherited it as one inherits one's blood. What I have determined through many nights of research and many days of struggle is in fact but a knowledge which I already possessed in a certain past life. The effort I have made was in truth only an effort of *unveiling* and not of acquisition. There is moreover no merit in this, because the reward goes beyond all suffering, beyond all effort.
>
> This constitutes one aspect of the question. The second aspect is *revelation*. Often you have used this word without truly knowing its meaning. Revelation is not an inspiration, a sudden bedazzlement. It is a true childbirth. Just as in the

case of the mother, the natural term indicates the moment when the event *must* occur, and it then occurs with all the pain of an effort *required* by necessity but refused, through inertia, by the body; likewise occurs the coming into the world, that is to say, the light of "revelation."

Revelation, you feel it coming, you know that the time has come when an obscure but powerful desire is going to realize itself, and you feel it coming through the incredible obstacles that life, that all the occult forces know then how to put in the way. When you have lived it, it is strange to look at these mountains which have risen up before you, especially to deter you from the event which wants to happen, which you desire and at the same time fear. Then comes the pain, that is, the hours of renunciation, the breaking of the I, the abnegation from all its desires, the offering even of its life to attain this instant in which the spiritual fruit will be born. And, again a thing you can hardly understand, you *are* the one who would thus receive the revelation, and you are also, like the mother, the one who is most ignorant of the nature and aspect of the thing revealed. It happened in more or less time, with more or less suffering, and you remain there, in front of the thing, astonished that it is there, uncomprehending even of its meaning.

This is the revelation? No, not yet. Now you must feed the child, learn to know it, study it under all its aspects, see where and how it is sick. One is so imperfect to give birth to spirit that the product has the risk of being utterly puny. You have so much wanted something, you are so much in revolt against the spiritual order, you have so much desired to be *yourself*, that there is a great possibility that the revelation has an organic weakness in its constitution. Hence it is now necessary to begin a real work which is a true motherhood. There, my friends, is what revelation is. It is not at all a fantasy. There is in all of this, however, something pleasurable, the sort of relief which one experiences after being delivered from a weight, heavy as life itself. You are different, that is all, but it is infinitely comforting.

So, one part of the doctrine is thus a revelation. It is the whole of this part that I call "initiation"; it encompasses the entire science of measures. What this means you will understand later on.   ("*Aor,*" pp. 77–78)

La Doctrine is a remarkable and densely argued philosophical document, one that gives helpful background for our understanding of *Nature Word*. Schwaller de Lubicz's procedure is to determine the simplest notions, "those notions which we cannot reduce, or imagine any simpler." He outlines what he finds to be the four major philosophical "problems": Existence, or *raison d'être*; Logic, or natural consequence (the development of the cause to the effect); Harmony, the vital logic of the cosmos; and Measure, or definition.

It is in his discussion of the second problem, Logic, that we find an illuminating consideration of the notion of *function*, which will emerge in *Nature Word* and other works as the keystone of his thought. Any cause, including the single, universal cause,

> includes, in itself, its effect, only this is not yet expressed. The effect is thus an *expression* of the cause, and this expression becomes that which we will designate by the notion of *function*. Now, function is action. . . . The cause is metaphysical cause first, and as soon as it enters into the way of *realization* of the effect that it *generates* it becomes *active cause*. Whatever the form of action may be, there is an activity which is cause. Now, the notion of activity is essentially linked to a representation of a movement of the cause towards the effect; whether the movement be quantitative or qualitative ought not to concern us for the

moment. One fact is certain: all movement requires a displacement from the cause to the effect. Displacement! It is impossible to disentangle the notion of movement from this notion of displacement, hence from space, and space defined by movement designates the notion of time. *Time, Movement, Space,* here are the elements of function, that is, of the development of the cause to the effect.

To the question of logic we can therefore now reply: *Logic follows from function, which is itself an accomplishment in time and space, hence in movement,* of an effect produced by an active cause.

We can easily understand activity, from the moment that we undergo it or that we observe the states that undergo it. In the beginning, hence in the absolute cause, there is activity. . . .

Since, in the beginning of everything, the functions of which we speak are neither situated, limited, nor conditioned, but are with the absolute functions, I come to the following: *Activity and that which undergoes it, which we know as resistance, are identical or of the same nature.* Furthermore, instead of saying Nothing-Cause[5] and Nothing-Resistance are equal, Nothing being equal to Nothing, X is equal to X, anything is equal to itself, we can say that anything is cause and resistance, and because the two are of the same nature this comes down to saying: *The Ego,*[6] *which is self-identity, is a totality which summarizes cause-effect, action-resistance, and, between these terms, also the functions or universal logic.* Ego as cause then means function and goal: Cause-action-function-logic-time-space-movement-end.

(*"Aor,"* pp. 84–86)

It is this understanding of function or activity as a

[5] The original Cause has already been described as "Nothing before itself."

[6] Ego is meant in the sense of any identity, including that of the universe as a whole, before itself.

primary term, demanding the necessary conditions of space, time and movement, and having an absolute sense as well as an immediate meaning in our experience, that should be kept in mind in approaching *Nature Word*.

In *La Doctrine* Schwaller de Lubicz approaches his major concern—the evolution of consciousness—by means of the fourth great "problem," that of Measure. Measure is not seen as quantitative, but rather in the Pythagorean sense of the definition of relationships.

> Measure is the precise definition of a cause to its end. Each thing, by this fact, has in itself its own measure, but this measure becomes all the more complete as the thing effectively summarizes the Cosmic Ego. What we call the form of a thing is nothing other than *the crystallization of the harmony of its Ego and its measure*. This comes down to saying that the determination of *the thing in itself* is its measure, the measure of its Ego, that which we will call, if you will, its consciousness.
>
> *Consciousness is nothing other than measure of itself in itself.*
>
> This seems very abstract as long as we do not allow the term of comparison to intervene. This is the case for the mineral and again for the plant. But as soon as we enter the higher animal kingdom, we see duality formed, in which the being becomes more and more *animated*, and is so, or appears so, because *it is capable of measuring itself*; in other words: *it becomes conscious of itself*, takes cognizance of its I, of its Ego.
>
> Thus I can say that everything has its own measure or *consciousness*; better still, everything *is only consciousness in itself*, or *all form is only the determination or appearance of a state of consciousness*. You will, I think, understand me and will eliminate for yourselves this antique and false notion of intellectual consciousness which is also called consciousness, but which has nothing to do with cosmic consciousness.
>
> ("*Aor*," pp. 88–89)

57

He concludes that it is consciousness which evolves, not form; changes in form result from evolution in consciousness on both the individual and cosmic levels.

> If we sum up for a moment these questions, in order to see more clearly the sequence, we find that the *raison d'être* is motivated by the necessity of the cause and the inevitable end, *immanent* in the cause. We find this end to be in *consciousness*, which becomes, so far as *measure of the Ego* is concerned, *cosmic consciousness*. And without losing you in details, if you pose to yourself this question: why are you on earth, where do you come from and whither do you go, you must then understand that *you are on earth by the necessity immanent in the cause, and you must therefore realize the cosmic Ego, the absolute I*, by the crystallization in yourself of absolute consciousness. Now, whether you want to or not makes no difference; you will do it through the experiences of your successive existences with sufferings which will be the heavier the more you refuse to acknowledge and work *consciously* for this goal.
>
> ("*Aor*," pp. 89–90)

Had the experiment at Suhalia continued, Schwaller de Lubicz might be known today rather in the same way that Rudolf Steiner is known, as the founder of a school of intellectual and psycho-spiritual development. But his life took another turn, and about 1929 the work at Suhalia came to a close for financial reasons. The next eight years were years of transition and further study, passed at Plan de Grasse in France and aboard his yacht, with two years given to living and meditation in comparative isolation at Palma de Mallorca. Forced to leave Spain with the outbreak of the Civil War, the family began its preparations to go to Egypt, which had long been an objective. Isha was deep into the study of Egyptian hieroglyphs while "Aor" was undoubtedly looking for the source and definitive expression of the consciousness and mode of thinking he was seeking to realize.

The sojourn in Egypt was to last fifteen years. Most of this time was spent in Luxor where, with the collaboration of noted Egyptologists Alexandre Varille and Clement Robichon, Schwaller de Lubicz undertook the analysis and study of the Temple of Luxor and the proportions, numbers and functions expressed in it and in its bas-reliefs and sculpture. Luxor seems to have functioned as a sort of university, just as Chartres Cathedral did in medieval Europe, and the very form and proportions of the building as well as its wall carvings contained information concerning the nature and destiny of man, to be transmitted to those who were trained to read it. Schwaller de Lubicz's unique affinity with ancient Egypt, due to his alchemical and Pythagorean background (both traditions having originated in Egypt), enabled him to uncover a synthetic picture of the epoch, the mode of consciousness and the understanding of nature and man represented in the Temple. In 1949 he published *Le Temple dans l'Homme* (*The Temple in Man*), a first account of the findings. Later, after his return to France, this was elaborated, with the inclusion of his comprehensive studies of the Egyptian mathematical and medical papyri, into a work of major proportion, *Le Temple de l'Homme* (*The Temple of Man*), whose first volume contains a thorough exposition of the philosophic basis of his work.[7] Also in the late 1940s came *Propos sur Ésotérisme et Symbole* and *Symbol et Symbolique*, both of which undertake to examine the use of symbol as a way and means of knowing, a cornerstone of his later thought.

[7] Sections of this are presented in *Le Miracle Egyptien*, a volume of selected essays.

As we shall see in *Nature Word*, a key to understanding the Egyptian sense of the symbol lies in the awareness that, just as the form of a plant is an exact response to the environmental conditions, both material and energetic, which formed it (its trophisms), so any object is the "signature" of the "abstract" functions which entered into its formation. The entire universe is the transitory residue of a certain play of eternal activities. Hence the careful examination of any object reveals the influence of the abstract functions or activities in themselves and thus information about them. We learn to read the forms of nature almost as hieroglyphic pictographs through which to perceive the nature of universal activities. What a stone can tell us of contraction or a tree's branching of expansion has an immediacy and resonance of meaning similar to that experienced in reading a pictorial form of writing. Such cognition by means of the natural symbol is the most concrete way of knowing, a process undisturbed by the intervention of mental constructs.

Schwaller de Lubciz's final book was *Le Roi de la Théocratie Pharaonique*, in which a wealth of further observations and reflections on Egyptian myth and symbol are given, many of them related to Hermetic processes. Here the mature philosopher's views find their demonstration in the Egyptian material, which in turn illuminates principles developed over a lifetime of philosophical endeavor.[8]

•

---

[8] *Le Temple dans l'Homme* (*The Temple in Man*) and *Symbol et Symbolique* (*Symbol and the Symbolic*) were first published in English by Autumn Press and have been reprinted (1981) by Inner Traditions International, New York, which is also publishing (1982) English editions of *Propos sur Ésotérisme et Symbole* (*Esoterism and Symbol*), *Le Miracle Egyptien* (*The Egyptian Miracle*) and *Le Roi de la Théocratie Pharaonique* (*Sacred Science: The King of the Pharaonic Theocracy*).

INTRODUCTION

The present work, *Nature Word* (*Verbe Nature*), was written in 1952, immediately after Schwaller de Lubicz and his family returned to France from Egypt. It was inspired, as we learn from the Prologue, by the answers, to questions within himself, that he received through the Egyptian symbols and the way in which they are read. On one hand, *Nature Word* is a summation of his philosophical position after its ripening in Egypt, while on the other, and most importantly, it allows us to glimpse the source of this philosophic vision, for its represents a transmission from one mode of consciousness to another.

Written in a single, uninterrupted flow of inspiration, with no rewriting or correction, the first section, "Answers," is an effort to speak from the level or quality of consciousness which Schwaller de Lubicz calls the innate "functional consciousness" and which the ancient Egyptians called the "intelligence of the heart." This notion of functional consciousness and the epistemology pertaining to it comprise probably the most important set of concepts that the author has contributed to modern thought. Many traditions speak of a "higher consciousness" and much ink has been spilled in recent decades in an attempt to explain such a notion, but Schwaller de Lubicz is able to convey exactly what he means by functional consciousness as well as to demonstrate its metaphysical basis and the method of knowing appropriate to it. This he does not with precise, logical definitions, but rather by talking around his subject, viewing it from subtly different perspectives so that the reader emerges with a deeper understanding than a sterile definition could give.

Functional consciousness is the mode of awareness which is in accord with "Nature's way of thinking." The text therefore takes the form of a series of answers given by

61

"Nature and her Sages" to the author's questions. The "author" is the spokesman for "persons unknown," that is, for the ordinary mentality of today, the cerebral-rationalist mentality which upholds the hypothetico-deductive method, the way of thinking which results from what Schwaller de Lubicz calls "psychological consciousness." Curiously, the questions posed by this mentality are not stated in the text, perhaps because we know them only too well, yet it is useful for the reader to formulate them for himself. (Schwaller de Lubicz remarked elsewhere that the answer to any problem is contained in the precise formulation of the appropriate question.)

A great student and lover of the Western tradition, Schwaller de Lubicz was also its profound critic. Yet rather than citing the ills of our civilization and proposing immediate panaceas for them, he sought beneath the surface of our social, ecological, scientific and artistic activities to find the underlying modes of thinking which have molded what we know as the occidental world. The fundamental error we have made, he says, is to have accepted a mentality which is in contradiction with "the thinking of Nature." We "granulate" into time and space what could be a grasping of a whole; we use spatial language to speak of nonspatial concepts. Our "psychological consciousness" projects its picture of things as a fragmented play of opposites back onto the external world and then takes this picture to be real.

Schwaller de Lubicz identifies functional consciousness as a mode of awareness and way of knowing which is accessible to us but of which we, as a culture, have neglected to avail ourselves since Greek times, when the habit of cerebral, rationalistic thinking became engrained in Western consciousness. (See *Le Roi de la Théocratie*

Pharaonique, ch. 2, "La Déviation.") In order to recover this lost "intelligence of the heart," we must, starting from the absurd point to which rationalistic thought necessarily leads, learn to abstract ourselves intellectually from time and space and awaken a way of thinking without antinomies, a thinking in functional identity with the thing to be known.

In order to understand how this is possible, Schwaller de Lubicz again takes us back to origins, that is to the One which is "reality" and the permanent source of all manifestation. Contained in the self-identity or "self-regard" of the One is the potential for all creation, which is actualized through the successive divisions of Unity into multiplicity. The One as the foundation of all existence and knowledge is irrational or unknowable in itself, yet, following its "initial scission" or polarization, the successive parts can be described in relation to one another and are thus knowable through proportion. The initial scission itself, a continuous and ever-present activity Schwaller de Lubicz stresses, remains a mystery that can only be described metaphorically, as in the creation myths of all times and cultures. Two metaphors were equally vivid for him: the Pythagorean metaphor of the generation of Number, and the Hermetic-Alchemic notion of coagulation, each of which, incidentally, plays a role in the Egyptian creation myths.[9] To follow the Hermetic-Alchemic viewpoint, creation results from the concretizing impulse, the "styptic, coagulating force" inherent in spirit, for matter, says Schwaller de Lubicz, "is spirit enclosed by the power of contraction which presides over density." This concretizing impulse,

[9] See Lucie Lamy, *Egyptian Mysteries* (London: Thames and Hudson, 1981).

63

the Creative Word, is identical with functional consciousness in its universal sense. The numerous functions that
exist, as we have seen, are the various kinds of pure activity. They are, as it were, the lineages of concretization, the
universal principles—sometimes called gods—which are
demonstrated in the transient forms of creation. The alchemists worked with many of them: attraction, repulsion,
polarization, coagulation, calcination, sublimation, exaltation, etc. Others we know from the more obvious of our
bodily processes: assimilation, elimination, respiration,
sight, hearing, etc.; in short, the behavioral processes by
which all things maintain themselves. "The gods are in
everything," said Thales in a statement that for centuries
has been regarded as enigmatic, but which becomes perfectly clear in this context.

The functions form the link between the Real and the
particular. Because the functions exist in us, because in fact
man represents a synthesis of all functions, he can recognize
and know through functional identity both the particular
instance of a functional activity and its general, ever-present
potentiality understood abstractly. This form of knowing
leads to a perception of things as vital processes rather than
as dead, disconnected facts: "Nothing is separated outside
of our senses; as a nebula gestates a Universe, so a woman's
womb gestates a human world. Function and phases are the
same: who looks at one sees the other."

Man as a synthesis of all functions can thus know the
forms of nature as himself. Natural forms (one thinks most
readily of the animal forms) are residues of man's own
evolution. The human being, Schwaller de Lubicz notes in
Le Temple de l'Homme, is the one evolutionary form which
has not fixed itself by overspecification. The various animal
forms have each developed and perfected a specific func-

tion—sight, for example, in the bird, or the sense of smell in the dog, or the power to leap in the cat—while man, though benefiting from the development of these functions, does not possess them in the same degree of refinement as the animal, nor is he obliged to continue exclusively with the perfecting of any one of them. Instead he continues to move on towards his own ultimate perfection as the synthesis of all of them. Schwaller de Lubicz sees "Cosmic Man" as the original pattern or seed of universal creation, as well as its final result. *The Universe is then identical with the cosmic nature of man.*

This notion of Man as Universe, evoked in *Nature Word* and further explored in *Le Temple de l'Homme* where it is referred to as the Anthropocosmic Doctrine, has been implicitly or explicitly at the heart of most philosophies known as "esoteric" and may in fact be what essentially characterizes that line of thought. Schwaller de Lubicz's development of the notion links it with the theory of evolution, first expressed in *La Doctrine*, whose premise is that it is consciousness which evolves, not form, and that changes in form are only expressions of changes in consciousness. Forms reveal the "signatures" of the functional activity which engendered them, and are the natural symbols through which we glimpse the conscious reality that they re-present.

The anthropocosmic vision recognizes the universe as a vast organism in gestation. The "creative Consciousness," according to Schwaller de Lubicz, is both creator and creation at the same time. Only the cerebral, divisive mind distinguishes between creator and creation. Yet, "God is not in everything, but every thing is a moment of consciousness of the divine Consciousness-Synthesis."

Time, he says, is the distance between seed and fruit. The

65

universal gestation does not take place in an abstract Time, but rather *is* Time itself. This conception of *Time as genesis* is essential in his philosophy and adds an important dimension to our thinking regarding this fundamental element of experience. Schwaller de Lubicz develops this idea in both *Le Temple de l'Homme* and *Le Temple dans l'Homme* in the context of what he calls "irreducible magnitudes," the terms beyond which one cannot go in describing fundamental realities.

In his development of the notion of Consciousness, Schwaller de Lubicz points to the initial specificity of things with their affinitive behavior (attractions, repulsions) as the "first form of consciousness." The process of concretization and individualization of the functional consciousness by means of a harmonic interweaving of affinities continues until its full expression is realized, that is, until each function possesses an instrument for its expression. Then a disaggregation of form begins, a return to the initial unity.

This vision of the evolution of consciousness, with functions as universal activities linking all phenomena, forms the basis of a philosophic position which has consequences in many areas of thought. *Nature Word*, for example, gives us not only a philosophic foundation for knowledge in which both a "natural" and a "supernatural" science can be grounded, but also a basis for morality in self-knowledge, and a ground for esthetics in the understanding of symbol and gesture. All the elements of a philosophical system can be found here, yet Schwaller de Lubicz himself insistently avoids all schematization and presents his thought in such a manner that it evades systemization by others. It is above all a vitalistic philosophy which seeks truth not in formulas but in the living, noncerebral apprehension of eternal invariables through their symbol-forms. Knowledge is therefore inseparable from self-development, that is, from one's increasing awareness of an innate knowledge. "What you inscribe in your brain dies with it." The "cerebral presence" and the psychological consciousness resulting from it must be surpassed, but this is not to say that Schwaller de Lubicz advocates the abandonment of intellectual activity. On the contrary, cerebral activity and psychological consciousness are indispensable and perform necessary functions which give us our distinctively human characteristics. But they must be properly understood and their activity limited to certain spheres. The presence of psychological consciousness in us signals for Schwaller de Lubicz a certain phase of the evolutionary process, in which Consciousness, having incarnated in matter, becomes aware of itself: it is the moment of the "reversal," the beginning of the return to the Source.

In *Nature Word*, Schwaller de Lubicz not only describes the general movement of the processes of evolution and involution, or becoming and return, but seeks also to enter into the inner workings of these movements, the mechanics, as it were, of incarnation, disincarnation and reincarnation, and the transmission of consciousness from one individual to another or from one species to another. In doing so he is aided by certain alchemical concepts, such as that of the "fixed point," and processes, such as the "exaltation of quality," for the alchemists, like their ancient Egyptian predecessors, were much concerned with just these movements. But like the alchemical writings, as well as the cryptic texts found in the Egyptian royal tombs, *Nature Word* indicates but never pins down or rationally formulates Schwaller de Lubicz's thoughts with regard to these issues, for they revolve around the central mysteries of life and can in no way be rationally explained. As he says in *Le Roi de la Théocratie Pharaonique*:

> Rare are the men who have been able to penetrate the secret of the beginning, but all those who have done so have, *by spiritual duty*, left a witness to the existence of this science, describing through enigmas or allegories—but especially through theological considerations—the process of work and the phases of becoming, without ever revealing the essential secret.

The alchemists wrote a great deal but never presented a key to their "Work," for they knew, and Schwaller de Lubicz would agree, that it is in the individual process of the struggle to know that the key presents itself.

DEBORAH LAWLOR

NATURE WORD

Some answers of Nature and her Sages
to the questions of the author,
spokesman for persons unknown.

I. The Answers

PROLOGUE

FOR A LONG TIME, often and everywhere, within the limits of my means, I have questioned Heaven and Earth and religious revelations and the words of the Sages of China, India, Palestine and Rome, but it was through the Symbolique of Pharaonic Egypt that I was given the truest answers, in my judgment.

These answers contain much that is known or obvious, but what is important is the teaching of the "Intelligence of the heart" that they reveal.

Does not Nature offer us through the commonplace all the answers? The senses which listen to them betray us. We must awaken the intelligence of Synthesis in order to approach the secret of Life.

I am attempting here to transcribe some answers received in this spirit of synthesis.

Our modern scientific knowledge [*savoir*] deceives and disheartens us.

The error of our world, is it not that of not knowing how to read the Universe as a concrete symbol of the abstract[1] sense of the functional powers which govern it?

---

[1] This notion of "abstract" may be approached through the metaphor of geometry. The relationship of the side of a square to its diagonal $(1 : \sqrt{2})$ is an abstract proportional law. It is unchanging and hence unmanifest; but its existence depends upon a square. The abstract proportion $1 : \sqrt{2}$ is the "cause," yet it is inseparable from its "effect," which

71

HOMAGE TO THE ARID SENSUALITY OF THE DO-
MAIN OF THE MASTERS WHO RULE HUMAN
ANIMALITY, WHO PERPETUATE THEMSELVES BY
SPIRIT, IN SPIRIT, OUTSIDE TIME, APPEARING AND
DISAPPEARING TO THE EYES OF MEN, WITHOUT
NAME, ANYWHERE AND EVERYWHERE.

ANSWERS

1. Son,
Because a glimmer of light has touched you, here you are,
overwhelming me with all the questions accumulated in you
from the long line of your ancestors and the experiences of
your lives. Please order the sequence of your questions.

. . . . . ?

2. Yes, it would be necessary for you to know in ad-
vance the value of the answers you anticipate. By ordering
the questions, you would be preconceiving the answers.
You have avoided the trap and I congratulate you. Obey

---

is the square. Without the effect the cause cannot exist; without its
cause the square loses its power to manifest itself. The abstract relationship $1 : \sqrt{2}$ and its manifest form, the square, are therefore inseparable.
The square may however be of any size but the proportion, which is
abstract, never changes. The mind, while seeking identification with
the abstract functional cause, must accept that its cognitions and percep-
tions are upheld and limited by the effect.   [Trans.]

the pressure of your anxieties and worries, they express your being. Within the totality of my responses everyone will be able to find some part relevant to him.

.....?

3. Let me answer your first question with another about your way of thinking. Why say "there was"? Why situate in time? Why compare?

.....?

4. But yes, you can understand without comparing; this is precisely what I can teach you, for each thing "is" in itself without any comparison and you must learn to think with the Thinking which is Nature. Accept this circularity: what was, was always so; what will be is virtually in what is, in such a way that what was "is" virtually what will be, and has itself only been the essence of the future.

What deceives you are the forms observed with your own means, and the frame of your limits situates things in the past and in the future and creates for you the illusion of a separation.

In yielding to this illusion, you are only able to formulate a science in which everything is "granulated" in time and space, in which everything is a juxtaposition of particles without connections among them. You must learn to suppress this frame of your limits and go forward, or to accept being thrown back, fragmented in a chaos of renewal, for you are the fruit of the last great cycle of "Becoming" on earth.

.....?

5. Stop talking of the "rational" and the "irrational": you only forge thereby the bars of your own prison. By this

method, which limits you to a dialectic of antinomies, you cannot even know whether you are or are not: how then do you expect to judge the Universe?

You are the Universe as the Universe is in the least bud of a plant. You may say that between this bud and its blossoming into leaf there is a period of time, and that this leaf grows, at each instant, by some quantity. What time and what quantity? Make your integration then with "infinite" times and quantities. Your logic leads you to the absurd and, note well, this absurdity is the door which opens onto Truth. Start from this "logical absurdity" and avoid on the contrary the science that leads you there.

.....?

6. Certainly, the "infinite" escapes your "granulating" comprehension; besides, you yourself are this growing bud, but by analysis you will only understand comparative forms and will never know this bud-leaf, nor what growth is.

.....?

7. No, growth is neither a succession of stages, nor an addition of parts. You can imagine definite stages when, in reality, in the very case that you observe, no boundary is fixed between what you call "stages." Likewise, tell me, what parts of the bud will you add together to make the leaf?

.....?

8. The leaf belongs to the lung of the plant, and the cells you speak of are functionally of the same nature as all the "breathing" cells of your own body. You look at the world through your senses, but it is impossible to have the Intelligence of what you have observed and compared

without the functional identification in yourself with the function revealed by the observed thing. If you wish to know Nature, see the leaf within the bud, see the bud within the sap, at the point where this sap attains its end as sap: its "absurd" point.

. . . . . ?

9. No, these are not words devoid of possible applications. Take heed: I do not deny the *usefulness* of a rational science, but if you want to follow the path which opens the Intelligence of things to you, allow me to lead you to the point which will be able to serve you effectively. Nature observes your science from the distance of her amphitheater, distant, that is, for you, but for her it all seems a comedy composed of tests in which she is made to play an imaginary role. It is not for me to speak here of your mathematics, physics, and biology, because, outside time, Reality—concealed by these tests which fragment—is simultaneously within Nature where Life is physical, which is a function of Numbers.

. . . . . ?

10. What does it matter if you see in these words a kind of metaphysical poetry of more or less "nebulous" theories? I advise you only to avoid comparisons because there is neither small nor large: it is *function* alone which is to be considered. Science, which objectifies, cannot know the individual except by means of the "large number";[2] and the

[2] The law of large numbers: statistics. For example: the colors of the solar spectrum melt into one another, no boundary allows us to divide them off. Thus ordinary color, red, yellow, orange, etc., is an appearance, a "statistic" so to speak, of each "imaginary section" of Red, Yellow, etc.

small cannot reveal the large, any more than the large can unveil the nature of the small. In reality, the causal function, unique in both, equalizes all which is All, without size or duration.

. . . . . ?

11. I will answer your question about what I understand by "function," but first I must warn you that your error, which is your downfall, lies in considering the "exoteric" aspect of problems. This is the cause of your individual and social ill. Before all else, awaken in yourself the faculty of abstracting yourself from limitations in time and space, so as to consider only the aspect common to everything and every living impulse. This applies more to your sensibility — emotional as much as mental — and even more to your nervous sensibility, than to either a particular emotion or a cerebral understanding and habit. By this means you will also be able to sharpen your relative instruments to do battle in a relative world. This latter will only satisfy the needs imposed by the contingencies, which are moreover illusory, of a sensorially artificial world.

I do not want, by means of sterile philosophical speculations, to lead you into madness; I want to show you, on the contrary, a real world, and then develop a constructive philosophical position, one which the so-called "rational" point of view will never allow. This last is a pessimistic way of thinking which leads you to uncrossable frontiers. What is "real" is outside time and beyond "Good and Evil," and not what appears in sensorial experience.

Understand me: the only reality in experimental demonstration is the natural general disposition of things, which you formulate — forever vainly — into Laws. This disposition is cosmic, it is alive in the Cosmos and is what I call here the Functional Principle. Some have called these Principles divine qualities, or even names of God; the ancient Egyptians called them *"Neters,"* a word cabalistically linked to "Nitr" and to "Nature."

Thus the "function" of growth is concretization of the abstract, just as the creative function is dualization of Unity, and all of Nature is the effect of Division.

. . . . . ?

12. Certainly! Mathematical thought seeks the general—one might say impersonal—formula. Now, since you understand this, why not apply this mentality universally and in a wider sense?

. . . . . ?

13. Yes, it is a characteristic of "modern science" to arrive at such "condensations" of thought and to work in the algebraic mentality. But I refuse to confine myself to "Quantity," to think only in Quantities. The *Neter* is alive, it will always act in the rhythm of its nature but will adapt itself harmonically to ambient conditions.

The *functional rhythm* of the *Neter* is invariable, the environment in which it acts is variable. Now I insist on a mentality that considers only the functional rhythm in order to encourage you to change your way of thinking and your attitude towards Nature.

. . . . . ?

14. Do not accuse me unjustly. You ask and I answer. Are you not in natural dualistic opposition to me? You and I? We shall only correct the error and be "One" with each other when our thinking is one and when every question

has its answer in its own formulation. This will be the true question and the true answer, and will be your deliverance. Nature's living question is only formulated when all elements of the answer are virtually defined.

. . . . . ?

15. How firmly this self-pride is rooted in you! As soon as an idea goes beyond objectivity you call it fantasy when it is not mad phantasmagoria. And yet, you believe in the possibility of radiesthesia, in animal magnetism, and you admit a theoretical condensation of neutron weight to a volume of two cubic centimeters for the total weight of humanity. You have glimpsed that the phenomenon which strikes the senses resides in the simultaneity of opposing principles of a thing or state. You calculate with negative values and "imaginary numbers" in the same way as with positive quantities, and you conceive three *aspects* of Nothing.

But, at the same time that you want to force the life of humanity into preconceived social theories, in reality you try to flee, you reject the absurdity to which your mechanistic rationalism leads you, and cover up your error through "mental games." You try by whatever means you can to flee yourself. And you turn to Faith as to a refuge, which inwardly you flee because it too you want to rationalize. Your debilitated nerves seek emotions in violence, to such a point that you debase to your own level the noble game of risk of elite souls. And in the end you tremble in fear before the logical violence your stupidity threatens to provoke.

. . . . ?

16. Which path to follow? The one that seems incred-

ible to you, that cultivates another way of thinking in you, awakening an intelligence without antinomy, and enabling you to find that state of "mental neutrality" which is the ground whereon pure inspiration falls like a seed, as the quickening morning dew falls on the fields.

. . . . . ?

17. No! Others preach to you, upon the basis of their faith, religious disciplines or methods of yoga. As for myself, I have to speak of this in another way. Following the teachings of the ancient Sages, what I have to offer you is a logical basis which, by means of a philosophy rich in analogues, can lead you towards Knowledge, because:

the same Cause, with different subjects, gives similar effects.

. . . . . ?

18. Yes, this is only a general principle, but Nature, by her signatures, will serve as your guide, because:

Nature obeys causes without deviation; thus natural effects reveal the character of their Causes through the Signature.

Analogies and Signatures are the Sage's guides and make him a Magus.

. . . . . ?

19. This word frightens you, but true Science is and can only be Magic. See how, only yesterday, your scholars were ridiculing alchemical theories, yet today they take pride in calling themselves alchemists. Your scientists, physicists and chemists have never been anything but disappointed and shamefaced alchemists. It is perhaps only through real suffering that you will come to understand the meaning

contained in this word Magic, which now only means
sorcery and superstition to you.

.....?

20. Oh innocent one! The Trismegistus is not a man. It
is the crown of the Sages, which the high crown of a great
pontiff still symbolizes today. You would like to make God
a man, and make a man of Hermes and of the Trismegistus
as well. Man would like to bring everything down to himself, instead of raising himself up towards the Universe by
sensing the Universe in himself. Your egoism comes first in
all your thoughts and acts, and you reduce the finest virtues
to your own small measure. Say: "Love one another," instead of delighting in yourself by saying, "Love thy neighbor as thyself." How can egoism engender altruism but
through opposition? You have turned compassion into
pity, and pity into the bondage of gratitude, and gratitude,
by rebellion, into hatred.

Evoke in yourself the suffering with which you sym-
pathize, and in this way suffer for your neighbor; thus you
will help and perhaps discover the healing remedy. Expect
your punishment from no one but yourself, because every
thought, like every action, carries its own consequences.
The justice of men is only a gesture to protect society: it is
not punishment. Let man love his neighbor, not as himself,
but in the *same humanity*, and so feel himself responsible for
and with his neighbor; because neither time nor anything
else divides the essence of their being. Zarathustra says:[3]
"Sun, what would you be if you did not have those whom
you illuminate?" And the Sun replies to him: "Fool!
Would you exist if I had not brought you forth?" This is

[3] Fr. Nietzsche, *Thus Spake Zarathustra*.

the pride of the rebel whose limited brain distinguishes an I, which it separates from the Self. Ra, the Sun of Nature, is not in you: you are One. God did not create you in opposition to Himself. He emanated you with his Breath. He is not in you, because He is the source, and you the flux which comes from it; you are One, and your separation is but pride's dream which would like to make you God. Zarathustra defies the Sun, believing himself Sun, against the Star. But can the fruit of the Sun be other than the Sun? The fruit of the seed is of the same nature as the seed. What difference is there between these extremes if it be not Consciousness? And this renews itself unceasingly until the moment in which the fruit and the seed are one. *This alone is the superman.* Meanwhile, there is false pride which results from the apparent distance between You and Me. I am teaching you the doctrine of *the hour of the dissolution and unification of "seed and fruit."* It is the limiting frame of your faculties which makes you granulate everything in time and space, and separate all into parts, without the connecting soul.

.....?

21. Function makes the first link, and Analogy, as the relationship of similar functions, is a second state of it. Spirit is immutable Cause, and body is variable subject. An old precept says that the Soul links Spirit to Body as the hypotenuse links the two sides of the right triangle, and by its squared surface, sums up their squared surfaces.

.....?

22. How can you take such pleasure in your error by still trying to find a chronological order for these principles and for the definitions of principal functions? When Spirit-

Cause and Body-Subject *are*, the connecting soul *is*. The one cannot be without the other. I do not speak here of "being," but of "existence." Now, you can refer to a functional order, but not to a chronological order, because between the polarizing function and the selective function—the first invoking the second—no time exists. Selection, which is the faculty of choice by affinity and thus *the first form of consciousness*, is immanent in the fact of polarization, which separates, hence distinguishes. Natural choice, by affinity, creates harmony or harmonization, which is the third essential function: it is inseparable from the notion of selection itself. It is this harmonization which, by connecting like elements, attracts and repels, hence determines and creates "individuation."[4] In objective, therefore sensorial and cerebral, application, there are periods of time; but in the totality of these four functions there is no separation among them. Now, individuation yields "One," that is to say a new Unity upon which polarization will become separation, selection become affinity, harmonization become fecundation, and individuation will be the fruit. In this way polarization becomes analogous to division, selection analogous to affinity, harmonization analogous to fecundation and determination analogous to individuation. *This is only an attempt to specify for you the meaning of the lines of analogues, at the head of which you will place a "Neter."*

You still need systemizations . . . but, as for myself, I apologize and humbly ask forgiveness of the Light of the world for seeming to formulate a system. When you are

---

[4] This word is taken here to mean the action of forming the *individual*, not to be confused with *individuality* which is a definition conscious of the individual.

wise enough, you will tell a story in which your Neters play living roles, very similar to those of men (because men incarnate these functions). Then you will call this a Myth. But nothing must be forgotten: And the surest means to be truthful is to be a Sage, knowing the secret of Genesis; that is, one must be a Magus, master of the Magistery of the three Kingdoms.

.....?

23. My answers frame your questions; and now you wish to know what the secret is and what a Magus is in relation to man.

I would have to pass in rapid review the principal problems of your science. However, first of all, and once and for all, in order to satisfy your troubled spirit, I want to make this quite clear: Nature is a succession, an expanded succession, in the spirit of the unique Genesis. This your objectifying thought can translate schematically. But I address myself to the being in you which is outside time, outside succession, beyond Nature. You can only realize yourself in immortality by going beyond Nature, which is the ensemble of the signatures or hieroglyphs revealing and transmitting the abstract characters of natural things. Concrete things speak to the form present in you, abstractions speak to your Intellect, which, outside Time and Space, is a unity with that which has no limits. Mechanical and mechanistic — therefore schematic — explanations must be *reserved to the Temple*, that is to say, must be kept by men prepared to know how to distinguish the true (real) from the false (the system). Thus Copernicus and Galileo were wrong in speaking publicly of the heliocentric, mechanical system, when only the geo- and anthropocentric system is vitally true and does not deceive people, but keeps them within the limits of theological revelation. People gain nothing morally or even scientifically from being no more than a speck of dust whirling in the Universe.

Note carefully my words when I insist on making you understand unsituated realities, because anything that you situate is no longer real, but only transitory.

.....?

24. Since you have understood me, I can tell you the secret exists. It is secret insofar as your consciousness is un-prepared to recognize it.

It is neither a question of a riddle, nor of a play on words, nor of any mystification; no cabala can reveal it to you, nor, especially, can your cerebral intelligence. Only your openness to the dissolution of your Consciousness in the spiritual Source, *which is itself the secret*, can reveal what is secret for you, cerebral man. I have intentionally spoken of *revelation*.

If you understand this, you will no longer speak of a history of knowledge. Inspiration comes at any time: revelation is individual. Only the method of transmission of Knowledge is variable, and conforms to the general state of consciousness of a people. The body of man is animal, but "revelations" occur and place higher consciousnesses in this body; because *consciousness alone evolves*, that is to say, enlarges itself, passing from a physical to a vegetal to an emotional consciousness, then to a mental, and, finally, by means of a mental consciousness of abstraction, to a spiritual consciousness. Your philosophy has remained at the stage of a psychological consciousness, the cerebrally mechanical awareness of true Consciousness, which is total and innate in the corporeal bearer, and to which the bearer and his psychological consciousness are obstacles.

.....?

25. Obviously your thinking is incapable of defining Consciousness, since you have not yet learned to read philosophy in Nature.

Assume as a condition (to which I will respond shortly) that there exists an indestructible milieu which supports the *inscription* of Consciousness; then, instead of considering only the brain, which is animal, you must consider the consciousness which begins with the first thing — I will call it the *"Nun"* or *"Hyle,"* but you may call it, for example, Hydrogen. This elementary body is characterized, and is distinguished from other bodies in the Universe. These characteristics are manifested by physical or chemical affinities. These affinities bring it closer to, or remove it from, all other bodies. I have already said: *this body makes a choice.* This choice is imposed upon it by its nature, it has no possibility of modifying the choice by itself, any more than does the lower animal. The lack of free will does not in any way deny the fact that we are dealing here with *a first state of consciousness.* What, then, distinguishes this consciousness — which determines and specifies the nature of a thing — from psychological consciousness? It must be a succession of intermediate states of an ontological evolution, of which physical expression will be only the physical instrument, at the service of an enlarging of consciousness.

To wish to find proofs of evolution by starting from organic evolution is to start from the wrong end, because only consciousness "evolves," or enlarges, and the physical — the corporeal — adapts itself to it. This is clearly to give to Consciousness the nature of Being, and to bodies and their characteristics the role of instruments at the disposition of this Being. This is the way to view Reality.

.....?

26. Your objection can be summarized thus: first, if Consciousness is Being, for which the physical instrument — that is to say, the typical things of Nature — is only a means of expression, why does this Consciousness not acquire its final instrument at once? Secondly, if this Consciousness, which you wish to confuse with what is called Soul, is All, why does it have any need to express itself? Third, how does this Consciousness transmit its instrument, since it is precisely this instrument which dies?

I will first answer generally: Consciousness does not need to express itself, therefore it does not need to acquire this formal or physical instrument. But if, for some reason, it nevertheless seeks such an instrument, then the answer to the third question will be: transmission is accomplished through the seed, which carries virtually in itself the form appropriate to the acquired consciousness which the seed will engender in order to regenerate the consciousness.

As for the uselessness of Consciousness seeking an instrument to express itself (which is one of the esoteric meanings of the Christic revelation), this implies an absolute determinism: in the Universe, insofar as it is our Thinking, a perfect end is foreseen from the origin, just as the fruit is "virtually" contained in the seed. Now, perfection is always what integrally summarizes all the functional aspects of a signature. For example: the right angle is the perfection of angles. A line, dualizing itself, opening to the distance of a quarter of a circle, but remaining attached by a pivot (the abstract center) to its beginning, forms the angle of 90 degrees which contains all angular possibilities. Thus, there is a "determinism" for angles. For the Sage, the path begins from this potential perfection at the time of his origin.

Understand me well: all perfection is the Unity of the

point of departure, the absolute Idea; but all manifestations — in the image of this Idea of perfection — *are only fractions of Unity*. For example: every angle is a fraction, or is composed of the fractions contained in a right angle. Starting from perfection, the Sage descends from the prephysical given towards physical forms; therefore it is necessarily upon the living, because acting, function that he must depend. Forms are then only transitory accidents, that is to say, moments of interrelation — or ratios — which are relative. For Consciousness, there are two possible routes: either that of the Christic or Horian Redemption, or that of the "Ancients," called the way of the "Good King" (Melchisedech) or the Osirian way. It is the principle of constant — or Osirian — renewal which requires the physical instrument of transmission.

. . . . . ?

27. Why this choice? Because there are three possibilities: either Unity does not divide, remains pure in itself, does not therefore multiply into its parts, and the Universe remains in the Cause; or it divides and multiplies. But it can also divide (take form) and refuse to multiply in order to remain in the image of the constant Unity.

These last are the Osirian and Horian lineages and the two principal paths: the Natural and the Supernatural Work.

. . . . . ?

28. What gives the "evolutionary" impulse to Consciousness is, in the first place, *the end desired from the beginning*, in other words: the finality necessarily implied in the Cause.

If no obstacle presented itself, this end would be attained

rapidly and directly. Now, what are the possible obstacles, if not the relativities of the phases with respect to one another?

Consider this example: the arithmetic series in progression from a unity of 1 up to 9 gives a finality of 9. This number is an end and goal for the series. But there remain the eight numbers which precede it and from which it results. The relationship of the number 9 with one or another or with several of these residual units creates multiple combinations, and, furthermore, there are eight numbers which can, for whatever reason, be the final number of the series thus arrested or aborted. Each of these numbers can be the head of a family. The simple progression will always be an uninterrupted sequence from the originating impulse towards a formal or corporeal perfection, after which Nature stops. However, residues continue to exist alongside this corporeal perfection.

If you now consider man as the final, natural perfection, everything peopling the Universe outside him becomes only a residue of his genesis; therefore, the functions which these residues represent are contained in the state of man so considered.

Next, it is obvious that man can place himself in vital, and also mental, relationship with these residues. His error begins here. In order to give you this picture, I have assumed that Nature stops at perfection, but in reality, two events intervene which modify this "reasoning": the first is that stopping is a death for the impulse, which does not however prevent the body from continuing to exist for a time with its characteristics, such as we observe with metals.

Without this stopping, it would continue to experience the impulse and the result would be the same for it as for any living thing: there is a limit of "density" (corporification) characteristic of every form, after which the impulsive energy is radiated. To the extent that this radiation can occur in a living body—metal, vegetal or animal—there is a possible passage of the corporeal, by means of energetic form, from one variety to another, then from one species to another: Consciousness evolves by enlarging the instrument for itself.

To illustrate what I have just said, observe that the wood of a plant densifies to a certain point which cannot be surpassed within the framework of its species. Thereafter, in the progress of the sapwood, the hardest wood becomes marrow, from which comes the mounting flux mixed with new sap; then, aired by the leaves, it descends again under the bark, on the one hand to be re-embodied, and on the other, to become the new seed. Its respirations then include, from the lowest to the highest, humidity, air, heat, light: the bearers of spiritual substance. Depending on the degree of subtilization of this circuit, flesh, seed, nervous flux and Spirit—mental and spiritual—are animated, from metal to man.

The characteristic of this vital play is *alternation*, because all that is moves and evolves by alternation. This is the *second* event to be considered, of which I have not yet spoken. Individual alternation is accomplished by regeneration through the seed.

.....?

29. The pendulum rises and falls. Thus it measures Time. Towards what does it rise? Towards what does it fall? What is the Time that it measures?

When the pendulum, the mechanical image of vital play, is at rest, it is in accord with the force which reacts against the energy which made it rise. The gravitational attraction is stronger than the energy which makes it "flee," but the two forces are of the same nature. This is the dualization of a single energy: one of its aspects dilates, the other contracts; these are the generating functions and this genesis is Time. In the end, if the contracting force prevails, then inertia has the upper hand; whereas, if the dilating force overcomes the force of contraction, it is the return to the origin that prevails. That is why the Sages' ancient precept says: "Flee from contraction, seek dilation."

But all life, all progression, like all propagation of Energy, is alternation, because what is momentarily determined, on receiving a new impulse, struggles against its inertia, wants to flee from itself in its aspect of mortal determination, and pendular combat takes place until the victory of one or the other aspect: the Sethian which imprisons, or the Horian which liberates. Likewise, in physics all propagation of waves occurs by alternation of "density"— at one moment dilated and at the next contracted — and appears granulated.

It is this contraction *against* the dilating energy in your nervous system that creates your emotions, it is alternation of affirmation and negation which creates your *cerebral* comprehension, it is alternation which creates natural evolution in general, that is genesis or Time. But this must be clearly understood: without the constant contribution of Energy nothing would live bodily. Predominance of contraction kills itself, but in so doing it prematurely releases the energy imprisoned in matter. It is the constant contribution of a new energy, in maintaining the living impulse until liberation by *dilation,* which prevents the energy so liberated through evolutionary return from remaining imprisoned in the Osirian cycle.

THE ANSWERS

Spirit eats the bodies which the Sethian function has made from Spirit.

Thus, as always, liberate yourself from what defines, imprisons, contracts; help your being to submit no longer to the pendulum of your corporeal return, and stop measuring a time, your time, your genesis in descent towards matter.

In order to help you better understand my intention in asking you to see things by and in themselves (hence to distinguish illusion from reality), I am giving you this explanation. Is not the goal of philosophy to seek Wisdom and to speak the truth?

Have you not noticed that your philosophers reason with arguments which rightly belong only to physicists?

For them everything is based on the trajectory-weight-time relationship, and their ultimate reference is ultimate velocity. This is mechanistic and not philosophic. Not knowing how to distinguish between these two leads your world to believe in "ever faster," an absurd motto which leads to madness. Reasoning with time as a limited value — which gives it a quantitative character in the equation — instead of considering it as a *generating function,* hinders the vital discovery.

In biology and in geology Time is made to intervene as the factor measuring evolution, when, in reality, *Time is this evolution.* Indeed, time is a fraction of *solar genesis,* which is the real, ultimate reference for man. Distance, measured by time, is specificity, because in a rigorously homogeneous and continuous environment there would be no distance, since each part obeys the same genesis; on the other hand, this environment, with respect to another — therefore through a separation of the phases of genesis —

causes a distance to appear, each of these environments having its own genesis.

Time is genesis, because everything, from the Original Cause to its "desired end," is in the process of generation towards this end, and undergoes changes, that is, it *ages*. Only the *passage of the phases* of this genesis is to be considered philosophically as *movement*; only *specificity* is to be considered philosophically as distance, and philosophically *Time is genesis*.

Specificity, being consciousness, speaks only to Consciousness, and psychological consciousness causes these specificities to appear as *objects*. Thus interstellar space has no dimensions, and distance alone — that is to say the difference between the "embryonic sidereal" states, the stellar geneses — shows celestial bodies as *objects* and enables us to define this "extension," to observe, understand, or acknowledge a path.

If the whole Universe were only this "interstellar state," nameless because infinitely homogeneous, there would be neither genesis — and therefore no Time — nor distance nor extension, and therefore no specificity. Should this environment divide, then two separate genetic phases will create Time, and two specificities will create extension or distance, and movement will arise from the succession of phases.

All life with its phenomena is only a problem of Consciousness. You distinguish one thing from another by its specificity, and it is the *communion* of your being in gestation with the state of gestation of the thing (an identity which awakens innate consciousness) which measures the vital distance you perceive psychologically as spatial distance. Thus psychological consciousness appears as the *reversal* of innate consciousness.

The path between these things can only be travelled by "some thing" and not by thought alone, for which Time does not exist. The moving object which follows this path undergoes its own genesis (otherwise it would not exist) which, measured comparatively, psychologically, represents a time, that is, for you, a quantity of time.

Relate these explanations to all sacred texts and you will begin to approach their intention. Likewise, consider the mental constructions of philosophers of your own time and tell them to call themselves philosophers no longer but to recognize themselves as mechanistic physicists. And when you study biological evolution through geological ages, do not forget that Time is genesis, not only for the terrestrial dust that you observe, but also for the Universe to which it belongs and whose consciousness is evolving, that is, liberating itself.

The dust you observe is like the living cell which is part of the living cosmic body, and it is this cosmic genesis that manifests life, the life you seek under the microscope in the part of a whole whose parts, in reality, are vitally connected. Do not commit the error of the doctor who looks for an amoeba in the intestine without taking into account the whole metabolism, from diet and respiration to the blood—the flux, its Nile, carrier of the impulsive energy of Life.

Everything is contained in the Universe, that is to say, in Man.

. . . . . ?

30. I still owe you an explanation with respect to what

fixes Consciousness. Only what you have "lived" affects
your seed. But understand this word as it is intended. To
have lived something is neither to have observed it nor
to have studied it: it is to have been emotionally affected, to
the point of undergoing a modification of vital behavior.

The most primitive consciousness is the "specificity" of
things, which characterizes them, and imposes a particular
behavior upon them. Only what has modified the actual
specificity of the individual can therefore be transmitted or
can determine a modification in variety such as the passage
from one species to another.

This alone affects the seed, and the "fixed point" of the
body through which reincarnations of acquired consciousness are made. But this only concerns the "specificity" or
consciousness of the physical being. Each body includes a
particle indestructible by putrefaction or fire, and this holds
true from metal to man.

. . . . . ?

31. Volatile bodies? Remember the pendulum: volatile
bodies always seek their fixation, and the liberation of Consciousness is precisely the possibility of no longer falling
back towards corporeal fixity, Consciousness itself becoming the independent, spiritual fixity. This, finally, is also
the goal of the Osirian cycle, a distant goal by this natural
path. As for the fixed point, since there is evolution or enlarging of consciousness, there is equally modification of
this fixed point, which however fixed it may be, will not be
so in the same way in the mineral as in man.

. . . . . ?

32. Where is the fixed point to be found? In the plant
kingdom it is in the ashes which always retain an alkaline

salt. In the animal kingdom you will find it in the bones. In man it is particularly in the femur, whence the ancient custom of crossing the femurs under the skull, in order to show and conserve, through the death of the body, the elements of survival and rebirth. Modes of burial by fire, air, water or earth indicate the esotericism of religious doctrines, since burial indicates the cyclic path the fixed grain is presumed to follow before returning to animate a seed which will transmit its characteristics. This can only occur through a milieu and in an environment which is rhythmically similar to the fixed grain, that is to say, related to it either physically or by tendency. This fixed grain is of a mineral nature. I do not say that it is metal, because metal has a fixed grain which is proper to itself and unique for all the metallic metals.

. . . . . ?

33. Certainly there are some pre-metallic bodies and other post-metallic ones, as for example, among the latter, Bromide and Iodine, which are vegetal products, and Phosphorus, which is animal.[5]

. . . . . ?

34. Leave to the physicist's study atomic hypotheses. With Nature look at the Sky: she ceaselessly draws from it that energy which physicists seek so laboriously in the utmost depths of matter. She draws directly from the "Nun," the infinite energetic Ocean of the world. And the infinite is only the undetermined.

---

[5] Present theories of atomic cycles in no way invalidate this assertion. Nature, throughout her kingdoms, accomplishes by simple means what has now been observed by means of nuclear "bombardments."

.....?

35. Perhaps one day you will understand these words, but regarding Consciousness you have well understood: in the spirit in which I have given these explanations, it is suffering alone which permits the evolution of consciousness. I say suffering and not pain, suffering in the sense of an event which must affect, impress your life and not your brain. Here you have the general rule for your existence, because your goal in coming is to enlarge your consciousness, your goal in departing is to carry away what you have acquired. The destructible body retains nothing. The indifferent acquire nothing. According to the degree attained, you will need action, more or less violent, more or less altruistic, or study, or meditation; you will need to seek either contact with things and people or isolation because, according to the *degree of the extension of your consciousness*, you will be differently affected in your life. So you must find out how to live intensely your moments of "awareness."

.....?

36. What do you want me to tell you of sexuality, this sex from which you derive your so-called happiness and your true unhappiness? Nature is the doubling of primordial Unity, its Yes and its No, its natural affirmation within its absolute negation. This dualizing function is the original sexualization exemplified by the Luminary of the day and the Luminary of the night. One gives, the other receives; one inseminates, the other gestates; each is itself double, it opens and closes, dilates and contracts. Contemplate this enigma: at the origin the One is enclosed, contracted, in the rising night; when next it reappears, it is in the day of Nature, having broken the "In-Itself" apart into I and Thou: this is the dualized, oppositional world, "the Other, enemy of the same," says the Philosopher.

THE ANSWERS

.....?

37. Your sexual behavior does not concern me. Morality is a part of your behavior towards yourself. What liberates Consciousness from terrestrial form is good, what contracts and imprisons in the body is evil. Honor the feminine because it carries within itself that which gives redemption, but beware of the female. Understand sexuality in its revelatory function, in its symbol: the attraction of opposites. Represent Unity by a circle: at the Present Moment, outside Time, a scission occurs and forms two streams: one goes to the left, away from the other, which goes to the right; each runs on a half of the circle, the Chinese Yin and Yang. On the opposite side, the antagonists rediscover each other and unite. The circle, or cycle, has never ceased to be, the scission has broken nothing . . . and yet here is the Creation, which is the *scission of an absolutely homogeneous state into two parts, heterogeneous in relation to one another.*

This absurdity is the Truth; attraction is born of opposition, and conjunction is the eclipse of the new moon which annihilates Nature and marks the return to Unity. But as long as there is man and woman there is opposition and enmity, and their relationship can only be that of copulation, whether physical, emotional or mental. Call this love if you wish so to name the *symbol of Love*—Love which is but the extension, the dissolution of all in all.

.....?

38. I am going to answer your questions by explaining a secondary subject. If someone were to tell you that mechanized civilization clouds the soul, this would be a statement without practical import. On the other hand, if I tell you that mechanized civilization clouds and even kills conscious-

ness, you will understand this warning: if you interpose between yourself and the object of your work an automatic tool which eliminates your will, especially your sensibility, all living contact between you and the worked material is cut off. The craftsman no longer "feels" nor comprehends the wood, the leather, the metal . . . his work is inanimate, it can neither emanate nor radiate any life, not having received any. You must then resort to analyses, to statistical studies of the qualities of the material surrendered to the automatism of the machine, because you have stretched a veil between yourself and the thing; however, the thing continues to exist, but you, a conscious living being, lose your life by stifling your consciousness.

Likewise the doctor, who ought to diagnose his patient's illness *sympathetically*, instead becomes a mechanic. Observe the phases of history: the most fruitful, genial and "living" epochs have always had a flourishing community of artisans. The Consciousness of a people can only be renewed through the crafts, and not by doctrines. Mechanized civilization is the agony of a world.

Specificity is the physical body's consciousness. Once defense by repulsion has formed by contraction emotivity, the first vegetal aspect of the future solar plexus or sympathetic nervous system, then emotivity becomes the second state of consciousness. When emotivity, by sensitivity to energetic flows, begins to *anticipate* the reaction, then the third state of consciousness develops, the immediate, lower, animal mentality, which will form what is generally called instinct.

Then the subtle matter of the Universe begins to concretize itself in the brain and localizes there, in the image of the Universe and its regions, the centers of *intelligence* which will relate to the exterior—by means of the senses whose mechanism develops through what in you and your being is identical with the Universe—and the revelation of an intelligence of Consciousness will occur: the cerebral consciousness of Consciousness, the psychological consciousness. There is a rigorous succession of evolutionary phases in the concretization of Consciousness. This sequence occurs alike in the evolution of a Sun and its planetary members as in the final concretization of the kingdoms up to man.

With man the *return* begins, the liberation of Consciousness from formal (or corporeal) contingencies, and the movement back towards conscious incorporeal Being, which is immortality. With the human being, Nature enters into the phase of material disaggregation. For you as an individual, there is that which precedes you individually and that which precedes you in general evolution, because beyond and greater than you are the *immortal Consciousnesses* of the Saints and Masters. Through Consciousness, the Universe is but one single thing; all is interdependent with all.

.....?

39. Yet this is not difficult to understand. You have two eyes which look together at a single object. This dualization of a single observation gives depth perception, that is the difference between distances, to your psychological consciousness. Most birds have their eyes opposed. Difference of distance does not exist for them, and by this fact their perception is "piercing," the object is neither far nor near and the "complex" of the cerebral intelligence does not arise to impede them; the object which they see is neither large nor small, it is. But, you will ask, how can the bird see an object with one eye while the opposite eye is seeing some-

thing else? What choice intervenes in this case? But don't you yourself hear a thousand sounds at one time? How do you select the one you want to hear? Ten thousand "consciousnesses" are at play at the same time; nevertheless, there is only one Consciousness. Ten thousand sounds at a time strike your ear, and you hear only the one that you focus upon, even when this is the weakest.

Enumerated force and quantity concern only your artificial being, your transitory instrument, your cerebral individuality. Only the Unity of your life, the Unity of your Consciousness, has a value. This is what constitutes your selective Will and permits the concentration of your intelligence, the synthesis, for it is this synthesis which is in the origin and which fractions itself into the ten thousand parts of the aspects of the residual Universe.

It is the granulation of sound and of all sounds which creates the mechanism of your ear, progressively, through all animal forms, for all animal types are only *evolutionary residues of the animal organism* whose "consciousnesses" are materialized, in complete interconnectivity, in man. One is digestive tube, another heart, another liver; one concretizes magnetic lines of support in the bones, another begins isolated tactile sensitivity, while yet another organizes a first central nervous system and so forth.

The world's *zoological museum* is ordained in the embryological Genesis of human consciousness. Touch creates tactile sensitivity, light creates the organ of the eye, sound makes the instrument of the ear, but it is the original synthesis, virtual Man in the *Fiat Lux*, who governs: thus the fruit, with the entire bodily form of the product, is ordered in its becoming by the form and goal *virtually* contained in the seed or gene of the chromosome, the *synthesis*. All these "instruments" or concretizations or incarnations of Consciousness are only stages of relationships, and it is Unity, the *Consciousness-function*, the synthesis of all possible relationships, which makes the Intellect and allows for the Will.

You see in the word "synthesis" the recapitulation of all the parts of an analysis. This is the error, your great error. Synthesis is the seed's virtual perfection, relative or absolute, *which is analyzed as it becomes body*. This analysis governs your cerebral intelligence; synthesis belongs to the Consciousness — of which you yourself are only an analyzed element — of a microcosmic becoming, of the Cosmos: the divine Consciousness. You will never escape the "vicious circle" of your mechanistic rationalism unless you develop in yourself the mentality of synthesis; this is a form of thinking which considers the elements of cosmic analysis only in the second place and which awakens, in the first place, meditation on the one thing. Thus the famous Emerald Tablet tells you: "That which is above is like that which is below . . ." and inversely. Here is your analysis; but this tablet of Wisdom concludes ". . . the one thing comes about through the meditation of One." Should one say "meditation" or "mediation"? See if they do not have the same meaning.

. . . . . ?

40. The proper path leads you first in search of your "Totem," that is to a *spiritual Heraldry*. This word "Totem" may be understood in several senses. I use it here to epitomize, as in a heraldic emblem: first the belonging to a principal functional line, that is a grouping of analogues; then, the recognition of the type corresponding to the personal signature, and therefore to one or other of the types of these analogies. A parallel may be drawn between this

101

choice and that made by the person "entering religious life" of a "patron" from hagiology corresponding to the signature of his tendencies and aspirations.

You cannot in any case step into the shoes of another person, for you are yourself a whole, a particular aspect of universal Consciousness. This Consciousness which is yours in the present is your instrument, but also your judge. Go and listen to this judge in solitude, for when you are alone, truly alone, Consciousness speaks. Woman fears solitude; this is why she listens to her instinctive emotivity, which is a counsellor for her and not a judge. Man, know thyself! Make this precept your coat of arms, and recognize your emblem. This will be your shield, as "cavalier" of the Elite, which will shine forth for the good of future people, as happened in the time of Pharaonic Wisdom.

.....?

41. Forget "elites" and recognize the true Elite. It is formed of individuals who have already gone beyond Nature. To be of the Elite is to want to give and to be able to give; it is to know how to draw on the inexhaustible source and give this food to those who are hungry and thirsty in the form which is suited to them. Altruism is the criterion by which to recognize the man who goes beyond humanity.

.....?

42. Certainly, this is not yet the last great stage in the liberation of Consciousness, but one must know how to stop and rest at the base camp before proceeding to the summit. Seek your heraldic symbol, the "Herald" of your Consciousness, and when you are exactly situated in the ladder of Consciousness you will easily see the next rung.

May the image of a footpath from the beginning to the end be sufficient to show you that each part, or what appears to be a part, is the Whole, and may you thus avoid the error of seeing the Whole as the sum of its illusory parts. The whole apple tree is virtually in the seed or grain, and you should not say that the apple tree is formed of parts which together make up the whole tree. Each particle of the apple tree is apple tree in its nature, and its fruit will be it anew, integrally, concretized in its *virtual* form.

I do not say "preconceived," but "virtual," and I do not speak of a "sum" of the parts, because the sum is arithmetic and mechanical.

.....?

43. "Virtuality," or the passive and "ideal" arrangement for a "determined effect," demands an active impulse. Thus thinks the rationalist who always divides. You, on the other hand, must not forget that the source of this activity is already contained in this disposition, otherwise it would not be a virtuality. This source of activity is a fire which burns its form when it lacks the nourishment to give to the vegetation which it has raised up. This virtuality is not an "image" of the fruit or effect. On the contrary: the psychological consciousness of the effect, which is concrete for you, is the transitory image of the virtual disposition. Yet you nourish yourself with bread made from wheat flour, the illusory effect of the virtuality of its seed? You forget that between your birth and death, you yourself are only an illusory phenomenon and that much time and effort were needed for your adaptation to "psychological consciousness"—which the newborn infant does not have. Now, illusion with respect to illusion is an affirmation, just as is negation of negation. You place your faith in this affirma-

tion to the extent of no longer remembering that the Principle alone is real. Hermes tells you: "The individual dies, but the species does not die." If you understand this to mean that hereditary continuity maintains the species, the statement is false, at least for this earth, because species disappear. But it is true that the principial conditions which have expressed a specificity cannot cease to be, because they are immanent in the harmony of the world. This is Eternity, a cycle which you would like to break in order to have a beginning and an end. And your philosophers pose a hypothesis for its beginning, a God outside the world, a God in the world, a world without God. Translate this word God as Consciousness and impulse, which is Life. The world is only this.

Admit a creative Consciousness: it can create only in and through itself. There is a *Fiat Lux* of light in itself. It is you, cerebral man, who distinguishes what creates from what is created. There exists no God *ex machina*, nor an unconscious God, nor the gods of your choice, nor no-God. You have prostituted the notion of God, you have made it an extrapolation for the unknowns in your reasoning, you have left the circle of Paradise. Your God is not in everything, but every thing is a moment of consciousness of the divine Consciousness-Synthesis.

To create is to think, but to think is not to create; it is, however, functionally and analogically that which comes closest to it. Imagine, if you will, deistic, theistic, polytheistic systems . . . these will always be only approximation.

.....?

44. Is there or could there be a philosophical system in perfect conformity with the truth? Certainly not. A system

is a prison of thought, Life is constant expansion. Formulation in words would be reduction to your own limits of what has no size. Only symbol, parable and hieroglyphic writing can communicate Knowledge, and whoever receives illumination receives it for himself alone, and anyone may receive this light. But the illuminated man, prophet or messenger, can never do more than indicate the way to follow, and one can only transcribe forever anew what these inspired men have taught.

. . . . . ?

45. Do you dream of marvels? Would you want to understand the language of the Spirit with your physical ears? But Consciousness, freed from its bodily instrument, can only speak to Consciousness, no longer having the instrument to do otherwise. Do you want to remain, when you leave your body, what you were during your earthly life? What you inscribe in your brain dies with it; you will remember nothing of what is no longer necessary in the new state, nor will you have the (cerebral) memory of what is definitively inscribed in your "fixed point." This inscription in the "fixed point," acquired for ever, will manifest itself by affinity, which will make your Consciousness move towards its like. Learn, therefore, during this existence to think in this "affinitive" spirit, rather than devoting yourself to the mechanical spirit of the relative association of heterogeneous elements, this rational *facility*. Leave that to merchants, who work with balances and require an equal quantity on the two plates of the scales, when in reality Nature appears paradoxical because the living reaction always seeks polarization.

Now, affinity increases with oppositions. Seek to know affinities by experiencing them through these oppositions, and this "sensation" will then serve as your impulse for true thinking.

.....?

46. What is affinity? Look at it this way: A falx, which can be seen as an equator, separates into two parts the cerebral mass where notions are inscribed. A *meridian* is drawn, represented by what is called the fissure of Rolando, dividing each part in two, and on this line are situated the centers of intelligence corresponding to the different parts of the human body: the feet above and the head below so that it is called reversed man. If we call the left part of the brain, as far as the equatorial falx (of the man lying on his right side), the half of the Northern Hemisphere, then the "head" situated on the Rolandic meridian is placed towards the North pole and the legs towards the equator. On the Southern Hemisphere, the same man will be the inverse of the man on the North side, with his legs towards the equator. I could have said these things to you more simply, but this image is meant to evoke an analogy in you. If you now interfere destructively at a point on the North side of the brain, you will efface a notion from your *psychological consciousness*, such as the notion of number or the faculty of counting, or the notion of name, or a memory: in a word, the *affirmative* notion of something. If you touch the corresponding part on the Southern Hemisphere, therefore, the right side of the brain, you will not efface any notion, but your understanding of the affirmative notion *becomes that of an animal*, because what constitutes the degree of human consciousness is the *faculty of negation*. For the animal, something *is* because his senses show it to him; equally for man, a thing *is* because his senses show it to him, but he has a particular cerebral consciousness of it

through the faculty "which is proper to him" of *being able to deny it.* Your intelligence consists in *knowing,* because for you what is can also not be. This is the ultimate comparison: Being and "not-being."

This explains what gives man his *instinct* for adventure: his taste for risk, his "instinctive" search to oppose to his consciousness of living, to his desire to exalt this consciousness of living, the risk of death. If, by means of the instinctive impulse of this higher faculty, you have known this consciousness, then apply this Learning [*Savoir*] to go further, and investigate the meaning of what, in phenomenal absence and functional presence, your senses show you. Note the sense of the verb "to know" [*connaître*]: to know Good and Evil, to know something, is learning. To know truly is not to learn but "to be with."

The extreme affinity is between "to be" and "not to be," whether the Being is the absolute or the present form. For example: Hydrogen, a fuel, has a strong affinity with Oxygen, as fire for burning, and, by this fact concretizes itself and is no longer Hydrogen. This is an image which shows how each thing, being specified, and therefore in an analytic state of absolute Consciousness, seeks to destroy itself in its specification, thus to annihilate this partial consciousness in order to seek one of greater extension. The first phase leads to an embodiment, the second leads (if it is, by the gift of free will, conscious of its real goal) towards liberation from bodily connections. This occurs by grace of affinities, which are only the appeals of Consciousness to a more enlarged consciousness. When the Moon is at the peak of her growth, and Eve, or Semele, provokes the male through opposition, it is in order to die in that which she is. Thus she involves the male equally in the death of the eclipse, in order to proceed, unified with him, towards a state closer to the Consciousness-Synthesis of the Origin. If you do not yet recognize the affinity you seek, exalt opposition, because this is, and can only mean, the extreme "affinitive tension."

. . . . . ?

47. Remember the guides I have given you: Analogy and signature. To satisfy your need for schematization, here is an image: in the same earth different plants grow; one and the same "vital power" will act on these different seeds. Obviously each species' seed will offer a selective *resistance* to the same "vital power" and will give different fruit. You can therefore infer the following generalizations:

The variety of phenomena is the result of a variety of resistances to a single activity. Determination, being a formal fixation of an activity or energy, will also create qualification. Determination is thus the measure of an activity or qualification. On the other hand, a total resistance against total activity will give the perfect product.

This image does not conform to reality: the "vital power" is not measurable because it is unlimited. Only the seminal resistance is limited. The conclusions, however, are valid because without the contribution of an energy, no plant could grow. It is also obvious that the nourishing Energy, as well as the *impulsive* Energy, requires a channel of adaptation from its universality which will be given by the intermediary "specificities," such as, for example, Nitrogen, Carbon, Oxygen, the phosphates and metals. An old precept says that between extremes a mean term is necessary. A single cause acting on different subjects produces similar effects; hence, if you give a universal character to this cause, the whole world will be peopled with similar effects, there will be analogy between all things. . . . This "reasoning" is clearly false since at the origin the universal cause cannot find its resistance—a seed opposed to it—except within itself, and this will necessarily be of equal value to the cause, that is, it will be the absolute Seed. This is the fundamental idea of Hermeticism, as of the Christian revelation. But in Nature the absolute original Cause is already *sifted,* analysed into ten thousand aspects or fractions of Consciousness, so that for *Nature* the cause is not the activity or original Energy, but on the contrary, the seed will play the role of cause. The seed selects from within its environment the Energy appropriate to its activity (reactivity). The same *seed-cause* will produce similar effects. The varieties of a single effect will be the signatures, not of the seed *but of the milieu* on which it drew. It is this vital, abstract milieu, the quality of non-sensible Energy, unknowable in itself, that you must seek to know through the *signature.*

. . . . . ?

48. This is obviously the source of therapy by "simples."[6] But in phytotherapy[7] all "reputable" remedies are not to be taken as they are, without knowledge of their signatures. You know that there are "local" diseases, but there are also characteristic plants in each place which play the role of "fixers," or "neutralizers," of these influences, and these plants may serve as remedies for men and animals. One should take either their flowers, leaves or roots and observe the date at which these are most active. Analogy and signatures will guide you. Notice furthermore that

---

[6] Medicinal plants, each plant being supposed to possess a virtue and constitute a simple remedy. [Trans.]

[7] Plant therapy. [Trans.]

fermented products are particularly sensitive to local energetic influences and can play the role of medicines.

But civilization has uprooted people. They no longer have their own earth and soon will no longer even have a country. Medicines are formed from products drawn from plants, from ferments, but above all, from chemical synthesis; they are employed anywhere for similar symptoms, and so-called scientific healing becomes incoherent, because each individual is a world in himself, rhythmically tuned to a particular milieu, and the same sickness varies according to the individual.

As to the influence of the milieu of which I speak here, it is that of the Egyptian *Min*, as *Ptah* or "Fire of Nature," the "Archeus." [8]

You have often been advised to return to Nature, but this good advice is generally inapplicable. To return to Nature you must first learn to read her teaching, and the form of this teaching is symbolic.

. . . . . ?

49. No, you cannot go backwards as the result of a single decision, any more than progress, good or bad, depends upon a simple act of will. You fall because there is a slope, you rise because an energy lightens you. But nothing stops you from directing your interest towards a vital way of thinking and a synthesizing mentality, without, for all that, going backwards in civilization. The errors contained in a civilization will be the cause of its own destruction. What it gives, or has given, towards the enlarging of Consciousness will survive in the resurgence of a true path. But be aware that in its action the pendulum that

[8] Paracelsus' "Principle of Life." [Trans.]

falls on one side rises on the other, and that, whatever its amplitude, it always beats the same time. The Sage considers only this equality of time, he leaves the fool to be entranced now by the rise, now by the fall.

. . . . . ?

50. I have said enough about what constitutes the "evil" of the West. It is to have accepted a mentality in contradiction with the Thinking of Nature. Nature's Thinking is the expression of Life through phenomena, engendered one after the other in an invariable functional order.

For example: Nature engenders through successive scission without isolating the parts, linking one specific moment to the next until the fruit is obtained. This fruit is the perfection of the moment and is a unity, whatever its name may be, like the foetal genesis of the chick in the egg, or the human embryo. You can therefore either remain consistent with natural function by counting and calculating by the function of doubling through division, or you can remove yourself from it by adopting a cerebral system of alignment, such as the decimal system.

In the first case, you will formulate a geometrical arithmetic; in the second, you will move into a rational serial arithmetic[9] which will be mechanistic. This latter method will be practical and will give results similar to the former, but the *mentality* will be far removed from Nature's Thinking. The vitalist mentality, which people take pleasure in characterizing pejoratively, is typical of Pharaonic mathematics. Its Sages preferred to maintain this more complicated method, apparently in order never to remove themselves from the guidance of natural thinking, and

[9] The term "arithmetic" is taken here in the currently acknowledged sense, corresponding to the "arithmology" of the Greeks.

111

therefore from Knowledge and theological guidance. Thereby they avoided the disastrous accident of the deviation towards a mechanistic thinking which occurred in the West as soon as the Greek *Diophantus* opened the door to the rational method, and to a materialism leading to a socialism whose false interpretation gives rise to a doctrine that integrates the individual in society to the point of rendering all possibility of personal liberation impossible.

. . . . . ?

51. This is an error: your methods do not give you any scientific advantage over the Ancients. For example: is there not indisputable proof of the Pharaonic Sages' knowledge of the value g [10] engraved on the obelisk of Hatshepsut at Karnak-Luxor? Thus the principle of acceleration was known three thousand years before Newton! Therefore stop allowing yourself to be entranced by the oscillations of the pendulum and understand the Unity of Time. Individualized Consciousnesses were realized long before you, and possessed a knowledge of which you still have no suspicion in your present phase. Observe the sky which is your great clock; all inspiration comes from it, because the World is only genesis within geneses, as the second is time within the time of hours. Coincidences, genetic accords and discords, constitute the true astrology. But understand me well: your Universe is Man. You yourself are man within this Man, as each cell, as each organ in you is man through you. For example, there is in the animal a heart as in yourself, but yours is a human heart, adapted to the state of your consciousness. By this con-

[10] g in physics, the symbol of a falling body's acceleration, is a constant: $g = 980.616$ cm. at 45°. The distance covered by this falling body is given by the formula $\frac{1}{2}gt^2$.

sciousness you are, on earth, in this Cosmic Man, in a determined place within his organic Consciousness, and with the terrestrial globe you voyage through his centers of life.

. . . . . ?

52. A literary image you think? Take care: this is not an image, but a reality. For you it is a matter of an image, a fiction, because of this damnation which always incites you to separate parts, to oppose them, instead of understanding their vital connection. If the Sages speak of man as a Microcosm, you immediately oppose this to a Macrocosm. This is the error: the Microcosm means only a manifestation, perceptible to your cerebral intelligence, of the Macrocosm; but you, microcosm, are in your life and functional organization one and the same thing with Cosmic Man. Your heart beats in a determined relationship with the systole and diastole of your Universe, a rhythm which is numerically in accord with the rhythm of the universal heart.

This explanation may seduce you, but this time in reality is only a question of an image since in fact no time separates you and the Universe, just as there is no time between the beats of a cell in the muscles of your heart—which make up the heartbeat—and the beats of your whole heart. The functional nature of these cells is to be "heart." The functional nature of your state of consciousness is to be Cosmic Man. So long as you judge consciousness as psychological consciousness, cerebrally limited therefore by the senses in time and space, there is necessarily separation between large and small, between limited and universal. If, on the contrary, you judge with innate consciousness, all limits cease to exist.

.....?

53. Yes, the brain is the laboratory of *Seth*, the contracting power, this Satan who imitates, or "apes," within a limited frame what is realized in the unlimited. Is this not the meaning of the function of "contraction"? Eliminate cerebral presence or hypnotize the brain, and your power becomes immense: your limbs no longer tire, weight is no longer a factor, you are no longer dizzy; your only judge is your present consciousness, that is, the actual degree of your innate consciousness. This consciousness is incarnated in your physical form in order to enlarge itself through the experiences which this form permits, and this will continue to the point of "spiritual experience" which will show you the moment when you will live, without physical body, the true, great, pure and blessed meditation.

.....?

54. Leave behind both philosophical speculation and belief. Speculation may be a guide, but it is a trap, and belief is most often cowardice. True Faith is certitude; when life conforms to Faith, it demonstrates the elements of Faith. This Faith of which I speak does not depend upon a dogma or doctrine, it has its source within you. All work within you and by you requires this Faith, which is the non-reasoned certitude that the goal aimed at is real.

.....?

55. No, hypothesis is a reasoned explanation. Faith is a mystic certitude, hypothesis is a rational artifice. To confuse them is impossible. Hypothesis is variable; Faith is a certain vision of a goal to be attained, it is invariable, it is like the pre-vision of the virtual form contained in the seed. The tangible realization of this form is a genesis. In its

114

ultimate image isn't this what your Middle Ages called the Philosophical Stone? Lithos, Petrus, Stone, because it is concrete realization in the most solidly material form; and "Philosophical" because Spirit is knowable only by Spirit. Let the imbeciles and the faint-hearted call your Faith Utopia and challenge your Utopia. If you die from it, what does it matter: you will have won by having dared to go beyond Nature, and this will be inscribed in your Eternity. Your West has lost Faith, and its clumsy mechanistic rationalism is everywhere in the process of killing this Faith, which I am here trying to make you understand.

.....?

56. If you want to put aside this vile and contemptible expression of foolishness which declares that everything must be of monetary value, then seek in the symbol of Nature the abstract Spirit which rules over all. Note: in the not too distant past you accused the Jew of being what you yourself have so awkwardly become today. But the Jew inherited something of the great Pharaonic Wisdom. The Jew is, furthermore, oriental: he is a gambler, he is also a destroyer. You have taken material values seriously; he has always played with them. You have destroyed without ideal; you have not, like the Jew, an unknown God, an abstraction, behind you and above you. But what can elevate, when misunderstood, can also debase.

Notice the devaluation of thought at the end of ancient Egypt's political existence when Rome took its place. At that point Mediterranean civilization took the wrong turn. Instead of valuing the joyful regeneration of the Osirian sacrifice, and passing on to the sublime, comforting spirit of the divine Horian-Christic sacrifice, men remained bowed down under the menace of an avenging Jehovah, the constant threat of the unknown having become frightening. They lived bent under the weight of their sins and crawled in shame before the abjection of their bodily existence. Men have never ceased to tremble before this redemptive death, and they weep at the death of the "Redeemer Word," which nonetheless unceasingly gives them Life, through which they are called to know Him.

The West understood nothing of the East as long as the East still had something to teach the West. The West believed in the definitive reality of values which are only tokens in the game of Life, within which even religious form should only be a token in the game. The West wanted to construct something durable in a see-saw world; and, seeking the durable within the perishable, it forgot the real, the indestructible.

Rather than losing yourself in "mental constructions," consider what is at your feet, what you walk upon: because "that which is below is like that which is above" — earth in the image of heaven. Behold the symbol in order to find the Thought. Look into the signature of the living in order to know its spiritual nourishment. Give to the Function the name of one of the living parts of your body; look at this *Neter*, at what it sustains itself upon and of what it is made. In this way man will know himself through his symbol.

.....?

57. Do not confuse Idea and Ideal. The ideal is generally only the egoistic construction of your dream. I am in no way an idealist and I am infinitely more positive than you. Try to be mentally as neutral as possible and then listen, listen with your ears to what your solar plexus, the detector of your emotions, says through your heart. Have you not noticed the Sphinx's large ears and how Pharaonic sculpture

gives its figures very large ears? What the ear—I mean the intelligence of the Word—receives, is not reasoned; now formulate what you have "felt," at least as far as you are able, within your limits, to "feel."

.....?

58. The individual necessarily abdicates a great part of his liberties for the benefits received from his association with other individuals. Social grouping is a fact whose means and goals are known, but it is a great error and a disaster when it is made into a state-like abstraction. One forgets the lesson of the so-called primitive tribes who construct their customs out of social necessity and not from laws enforced by police constraint. But you are in this milieu which today intimidates your free life; this is the reason for choosing, apart from your utilitarian obligations, an intellectual or practical work, to which to consecrate *your love* and hours of liberty. Work with love then and you will learn that if woman loves the fruit of her work, man loves the work of the fruit.

Apply true principles to your work, and your progress, not the appreciation of your peers, will be your reward. When the fruit of your work is ripe, disown it, because it is the effort and the consciousness acquired which are of real value and not the materialized object. Apply the acquisition of your consciousness to a new goal. Is this not what you do continually—but unconsciously—throughout your incarnations? Do it consciously in this life, in order to progress more quickly. In this way, you will apply, in its true sense, the principle of "constant revolution."

.....?

59. I see that reading and "hearsay" concerning the

knowledge transmitted by India leaves your awakened curiosity unsatisfied. But how can I speak intelligibly to you of the Man-King? It has to do with the mystical realization of man. This "King" presents at least two aspects: the perfect heraldic realization of a lineage and the incarnation of the perfection of the consciousness of his time. To understand the Man-King is to understand the subtilizing regenerations of Consciousness, represented by the phases of disincarnation, a sort of "dis-envelopment" of the "chrysalid consciousness" of increasingly immaterial bodies, up to the complete and *conscious* liberation of Consciousness. The Man-King is the *hieroglyph* of the regenerative death of a perfection achieved by Nature: he is a king, just as gold, for example, is the king of metals. In the Christian revelation, the Messenger King must die as such: He returns to the Origin which has emanated him, before "woman" may touch him anew, that is to say, reincarnate him. So the Gospel understands it.

The history of subtle lives is the history of the return of Consciousness, after having lived all aspects virtually immanent in the Creative Unity. For you, this is a kind of "story," a schema of analyzed elements; but in reality, the *time* of your cerebral imagination does not exist in the other world, the Egyptian *Dwat*, any more than it does between the moment you go to sleep and when you reawaken. For man death is only a cerebral and physiological sleep and, in general, for all of Nature, it is only a sleep of perishable elements. The duration of this sleep exists only for those who, cerebrally awakened, observe it. It is therefore here below, in your present form and by the extension of your consciousness, that you can prepare for what will happen following your actual death. And know that, if you accept it, death is not painful. Note that man's greatest physical delights are associated with the *natural* fact of the renunciation of physical life: sleep, dangerous adventure, coitus, death. Only the "hanging on" to what one is leaving, like personal love, hate, wealth and all regrets, makes death painful.

Your free will, subtractive as it is, must serve you in the accomplishment of your work.

. . . . . ?

60. You are not a creator. Your free will can only break down what is there, then make a choice between the pieces so as to reconstitute them into an artificial whole. This is the "subtractive" nature of free will: it can only subtract, and must subtract before being able to choose. Your free will is quantitative, that is, cerebral. You can kill yourself, but you can not give yourself life. Pure and true free will begins only when Consciousness can choose without judging, hence without mental intervention.

. . . . . ?

61. Renounce? You have often been advised to renounce. But I tell you: renounce illusion, but for God's sake, do not renounce Life! This Life was given to you as your lesson; therefore take the lesson, which is to search for the Real through the symbol of the relative.

In order to separate the true from the false — whether they be absolute or relative — a mean term is needed which can be divided and whose affinity moves towards one or the other of the opposites. In the intellectual domain this mean term is scientific verification. In the psychological domain, which interests us here, the mean term is verification by what I call "naked rawness." Let no false modesty, which might lead to *Amorality,* hinder you when you come to

119

judge your own reactions in the face of the bare rawness of things and of yourself. Always consider that conscious immorality is infinitely better than amorality, this inertia of the moral sense that destroys conscience. Do not confuse morality with the moral sense. The moral sense is the word of the supreme high judge within you. Its judgment is not reasoned, it is limited only by the state of your present consciousness. Symbol and moral sense must be distinguished. The natural symbol is the synthesis of a group of vital functions. The corn poppy in the fields is the symbol of the season and the vital conditions in its environment, and the sexual behavior of man is the symbol of his race. Woman's preoccupation with clothing and food is the symbol of her destiny which is to clothe with flesh the Consciousness-Soul, and to nourish it. *The symbol guides you in your objective judgment, the moral sense judges you in your subjective judgment.*

. . . . . ?

62. But applied "morality" is always a constraint, it should be used to acquire the mastery necessary for the accomplishment of the human work. It should never be, or become, an "inhibition." Morals were *formulated* as a means of defense, so that you could use them as instruments for mastering the appeals of inertia and the inclination towards the corporeal.

. . . . . ?

63. As for the sexual education of the young, note: the shame which is attached to sexual questions is above all an erotic problem and not a physiological question.

The erotic is a *psychological power* independent of seasonal rut (animal), reserved to humanity, in whom evocation by words, images — and in general by the imagination — can provoke sexual power or need at any time.

It is the consciousness, even if unformulated, of this erotic power that renders the sexual education of children difficult.

The man who is primitive, or close to animality, experiences little of this eroticism, whose power increases with the evolution of consciousness and the consequent enlargement of the "moral sense."

The easier the "moral shock," the more the "moral sense" is developed and "sensitive," the greater the erotic power. This is coupled with the weakening of the animal nature of the sexual powers.

.....?

64. After having summed up my answers, your final question concerns matters which go beyond Nature. From the beginning of time humanity has tried to answer these questions concerning a supranatural science. Your present science, covering itself with a rational-scientific screen, has only one desire, which is to circumscribe the irrational aspect it knows to preside over all. You know very well today that, in the intellectual domain, the mathematical balancing of equations in a single solution can no longer suffice: reversibilities and indeterminacies now enter imperiously into mathematical reasoning. You have admitted into practical consideration the absurd "speed of light" as a system of reference, a new "Euclidian absurdity of the point." You will not break the vicious circle of deterministic rationalism without falling into a new nothingness from which only the discovery of Nature's symbols can save you. And manifested Nature begins and ends, a fact upon which reason can rest. Where it begins it is much closer to

the original Cause, and where it ends it returns to this
Cause. Between the two extremes there is Life, and Life is
only a ferment (the *hek* scepter, the Pharaoh's crook), a ferment that fixes the causal Energy (the *nekhekha* scepter,
principle of reactivity) which causes the appearance of the
active Fire (*Min*) of the Ferment.[11] This is the universal
function, by which the supranatural becomes natural, until
it once again goes beyond the natural, having acquired consciousness of the divine Consciousness which manifests
Nature. But: "Unction shows the direct path through the
general death of Nature." This is the Rosicrucian's
enigmatic answer. It is an immortal truth, but its expression is outdated.

Yesterday humanity understood only through juxtaposi-
tions of the tangible, today it begins to think in non-
objectivized ideas. It already glimpses the Universe as an environment of "energetic fields"; tomorrow, it will even
forget the electric and magnetic sources and will see these
"fields" no longer as results, but as the Causes themselves.
Then, for certain people, there will occur the illumination
necessary for a science of Genesis, in which the greatest
power of the World, in sweetness and in love, becomes
conscious of the Whole, cursing the violence of the
"Sethians," who must smash in order to find a fraction of
this power that "God freely gives them" as the Ancients'
formula says.

Be clear about this: the essence and key of all science,
whether theological, medical, physical, chemical, in fact of
all science which is not just classification, is the problem of
the "nucleus," that is to say: the styptic coagulating force
of Spirit, or metaphysical substance, in corporeal matter,

[11] Called Archeus [the central fire] by Paracelsus.

122

for Matter is Spirit enclosed by the power of contraction which presides over density.

Nuclear science has made this image familiar to you, but I could just as well have spoken to you of the "fragrance" of God, as did the Pharaonic Sages, or of the "divine Will" and of the Will in general, or of the *Fiat Lux* of Genesis, or of the scission of Unity.

This is the supranatural Science which constitutes Knowledge.

. . . . . ?

65. If this high science demonstrating Spirit—BA and KA, that is to say the soul and what holds Soul and Spirit together (that which is all One)[12]—did not exist, then all the sacred texts would be only misleading speculations.

Then I formulated this question:

"How can I believe in such a Science as the key to Knowledge, since I am of Nature, in Nature, and in order to "see and touch" I would need, as an intermediary, at least a tangible form, though this be the first that material evolution can offer?"

I was answered by the silence of Harpocrates.

•

---

[12] Cf. Isha Schwaller de Lubicz, *Her-Bak, Egyptian Initiate* (New York: Inner Traditions International, 1978), ch. XII–XVIII.

Epilogue

Unity or Multiplicity of Causes?

Unity is in the creative function, being, multiplicity is in Time, existence. At each instant nebulae are born, embryos of worlds in gestation, just as, in the image of worlds, embryos are gestated in the female womb.

Dates and ages juxtapose themselves, superimpose themselves, conflict and agree.

Multiplicity in disorder creates Harmony through affinity, because complements agree with one another, antipathies repulse one another, creating the harmonious order of worlds.

The generating function is one; Harmony effaces multiplicity, the discord of Times.

Unity reigns and it is impossible for it not to reign, even when the Archangel Space separates in order to create intelligence. Space separates above from below, beauty from ugliness, day from night, it fractions Unity, it shows worlds separated by an infinity which thrusts unbearable anguish into the heart of man. The anguish is the consciousness of mental illusion.

Nothing is separated outside of our senses; as a nebula gestates a Universe, so a woman's womb gestates a human world. Function and phases are the same: who looks at one sees the other.

Eternal Present and Succession?

Creation is the self-scission of a homogeneity into parts heterogeneous in relation to each other. This creates Space.

124

Causal Energy, the absolute homogeneous environment, is inexhaustible, and scission obeys no reason. Creation is continuous, past and future are joined in an eternal Present. Cause and Finality, separated by Space, are reconnected by Time, which measures Space. Succession is made of units of Time. This is the illusory "granulation" of the cerebral mind. The finality defines the Cause, but in the Cause the finality is virtually contained: it is therefore temporal form which granulates, and we know that it is destructible. Space is our cerebral separative action, it is the illusion which makes identity impossible for our senses.

Magic, however, has its source in identity, because two identical things are no longer two, but one and the same thing: what the one undergoes, the other undergoes likewise.

This is the "magic" symbol of the "Miracle of the one thing."

The Perennial Character of Knowledge

Knowledge has never been lost and never will be lost. Knowledge is not a *thing* which can be destroyed or lost. It has its source in Consciousness and receives its inspiration from cosmic Consciousness, and can be betrayed neither by writing nor by words. It is not a mere science to be transmitted. When conscious experience has enlarged Consciousness in a being of real humility, then the prayer of the desire to know can provoke the spark of the sacred flame, which will grow into the fire of the desire for Knowledge. This divine fire will burn away painlessly the weaknesses and passions that others rightly, and sometimes successfully, seek to conquer through self-criticism and medita-

Manuscript sheet in author's hand. "The Passage of Consciousness." English translation opposite.

tion: on the condition that one does not seek "powers."

In the Light of Knowledge, all the Sages and Magi of all the racial phases of humanity's embryology come together, whether they be black, white, yellow or red.

The Passage of Consciousness

Form is the crystallization of specificity. Specificity cannot change without destruction of form. This is the "work of Life," that is to say destruction through natural decomposition and reorganization, or reconstitution, of a new form.

This reconstitution requires a ferment which is seed. This ferment is the "fixed point," which is the essence or center of everything. Through corporeal life, between birth and death, influences (or sufferings) can modify this fixed center, and this will, at the time of reconstitution, modify the specificity. This creates "evolution." Thus evolution can only be produced by "suffering," that is to say, profound affectation, inscribing itself in the "fixed point" (the indestructible nucleus), whether this be in an organized being or an inorganic thing.

Is God Immanent or Transcendent?

Neither the one nor the other.

Immanence and transcendence exist only for the antinomial cerebral intelligence. To speak in the tradition of Moses: this duality only begins with the expulsion from Paradise. The entrance to this Paradise is guarded by the Archangel with the flaming sword, at the Eastern gate where the Sun rises, separating Night from Day.

Today we are at the West, the extreme West, where the Sun sets, where Fire returns to Water and Day is once again wedded to Night.

St. John the Baptist's Day, 1952

II. Reflections

NATURE had shown me a great mountain, crowned with a peak of immaculate whiteness, but she was unable to teach me the way leading to it.

I had to seek beyond Her.

It was a long search.

We sleep or we are awake. We ascribe all value to the waking state, in which our senses show us the exterior world as *real*. Our senses inform us of objective existence. Whom or what do they inform? Necessarily that which in us, in some way or other, coincides with the object, identifies itself with it through what essentially specifies it. What essentially specifies the variety of things is their behavior towards one another through their affinities, which constitutes an activity. Such "activities" must be innate in us so that their coincidence with sensorial information about what is exterior to us can make us psychologically understand it. This is called *having consciousness of* . . . Thus, one can generally speak of an *innate consciousness* and of a *psychological consciousness*, the latter resulting from a coincidence of the former with sensorial information. To be *awake* then means: to have excited the innate consciousness, that is to say an activity which is innate in us.

Which of these two aspects is Real? The object and its characteristic activity, or this innate activity within us? Necessarily it is the activity in itself, whether it belongs to the object or to our being.

Each simple thing in the Universe, like each living organic thing, represents, *as an individual*, a finality, whether it is the individual Lead among metals or the individual Man among organized beings. *The finality consists of the sum of the innate activities.*

We do not know all the *possibilities* of "activities." Our mental knowledge is limited, not by the "possibilities" but by the objective existence of which the senses can inform us. As the complete, present, finality, Man of necessity must carry, innately within him, the sum of all the activities of the Universe which he recognizes. This means that he has within himself all *present* realities. With respect to his psychological consciousness, these realities express themselves either "a priori" or as "intuition," or, lastly, as rational certitudes. The latter are relationships more or less defined by "sensations." Sensations are the foundation for the dialectic by which the exterior imposes itself upon us as Real, whereas true Reality is activity in itself. The illusion of objective reality, which is the error of our thinking, should therefore cease as soon as we succeed in *vitally experiencing* the activity, without seeking a definition, eliminating thereby a dialectical knowledge between ourselves and object.

Now any philosophy of knowledge is dialectical, beginning with the analysis of our sensation of Space. The newborn infant is Space, but a long education — through the senses — is necessary for a psychological consciousness to be formed of the location of objects, and therefore of a concept of space. To incarnate is synonymous with "to singularize oneself objectively."

Singularization is a personal, that is to say particular, characteristic definition, not to be confused with any other. In incarnating, Being leaves Universality, is enframed within the limits outlined by the senses.

Now the senses are the effects of activities and correspond to *a mean* of their energy. If the senses corresponded to the totality of an activity's energy, they would no longer be restrictive, and there would be an *identity* between the exterior activity and the innate activity, a union, hence a cessation of an "exterior" with respect to an "interior": light would be total, encompassing all vibratory possibilities, causing the differentiation between innate light and apparent light to cease.

The sensorial instruments for the senses of touch, smell, sight, taste, hearing, are all *mechanical* organisms; that is they are functionally limited to a limited mechanical power, partially corresponding to universal energetic influence.

The functional reaction of the same innate energy is equal to the action — or function — of the senses. All observation of activities beyond the sensorial limit requires an instrumentation which brings it to this limit. What calls forth this ingenuity in us is the knowledge of the innate activity, which is itself unlimited. This knowledge is the Intellect, from which our understanding of the reaction to the activity of the sensorial mechanisms results. This is no longer a *sensation,* but an *experience.* Sensation is caused by the exterior; experience is inner, a *reaction* of innate activity.

A function of something exterior to us can be experienced functionally within us. This is an identification, a "union" of our Being with the being of anything. By this means we can escape the limitation imposed by the senses and Know [*Connaître*], instead of simply being informed [*savoir*].

This is the way which leads to the immaculate peak.

•

Incarnation, in general, appears to be the concretization (or coagulation) of a power, at whatever degree of abstraction, enabling the same concrete state of the Universe's activities or functions to be known. For example: fluid knows fluid, solid knows solid and psychic knows psychic—because our physical *form* is only one aspect among other *forms*, that is, other *concretizations*. The Universe is a simultaneity of all Worlds.

For our physical incarnation, physical form is the lowest state of concretization, and is symbolized by the idea of the stone. All other less physical (less concrete) states are contained in this "stone." The man who, by *experience*, can identify himself with the psychic will see, hear, touch everything within this psychic world, after which the corporeal will become penetrable for him. Many simple people, unclouded by the "dialectic" of the senses, are capable of transporting themselves into this psychic world, especially if by means of rituals they plunge into a state suppressing all cerebral control.

Objective reality is absolutely relative. It is the effect of functional coincidences and is subordinated to the limits of the senses. *Incarnation* can be designated as a present state of concretization whose form is governed by function.

In our incarnation the concrete is what is physical, because our form knows only the physical state, which is the lowest, most corporeal state of our Being. Our "physique" or *body* is, however, composed of all other states of concretization, not as parts linked to one another but as an interpenetrated whole. Thus our psychic *form* is made of the same substance as our physical form, but according to a different spatial law. Now, we have extended the notion of space to a fourth dimension, but this is only a mathematical game and a transference of what we can understand into an abstract domain which is purely symbolic. We analyze cerebrally, rationally, but, in reality, it is a question of another state of life. We can schematically define an ordinary three-dimensional volume and calculate it with the coordinates x, y, z. However, the locations x, y, z are only *mathematical points*, and all paths as well as any form drawn by these points are only diagrams composed of hypothetical points. Functional volume escapes cerebral comprehension; we are unable to *experience* it rationally. In order to *experience extension* in three dimensions, we must transfer ourselves into another state of consciousness, eliminating *cerebral control*. For a cube to increase by any quantity in a cubic manner, it must grow not only in terms of its faces, but also of its edges and apices. Now we can experience this, growing cubically with the cube, on condition *of no longer sensing it objectively*. We must be cube in the cube.

It is not a question of looking cerebrally for extravagant conclusions, but, on the contrary, of solving the most immediate problems by awakening the *consciousness corresponding* to the nature of the thing to be known.

Qualitative appearances belong to sensory information, hence address themselves to cerebral analysis. Function, on the contrary, is innate in us, since our corporeal, physical form results from it. We can experience function, we can *imitate* it, even the function of extension in volume, which is what we do in breathing.

But it is not only a question of movements: these can

133

mislead us for they too readily invite analysis into components. Within movement, which is mechanical, we must see the *gesture*, which is vital. The yawn, for example, reveals the secret of *Aum, mane padme h'mm*, which we find again in the Islamic *Moham'med* and elsewhere under many other forms. The *gesture* which accompanies the word is always accurate in its meaning, the inverse is very difficult and requires reasoning.

There is no secret which is not revealed by a natural gesture of the human body.

Knowledge is innate in man because he is the present final product of all activities, in other words, of all functions. This is the foundation of ritual gestures, and it would be an error to wish to find their meanings in rational speculations, or in *cerebral analyses*.

There are many gestures of blessing, for example, and one must execute them oneself to experience them instead of reasoning about them.

But each thing has its proper gesture, its function, from the mineral to the vegetable, from the vegetable to the animal, from the animal to man.

The Universe is wholly activity.

Know the Universe through man in order to discover finally conscious repose, divine serenity, the serenity of the Sage or Saint, Lao Tzu would say.

If you want to know the character and basis of thought of a person with whom you are speaking, imitate his carriage, his gestures, his facial expressions. He who by nature hides his thoughts will be "cold," very sober of gesture and will have no lines on his brow. Oh the dangerous, beautiful, smooth face! But it is useless to imitate gesture with physical gesture: it is enough to close one's eyes and to "live" it, to experience it without movement, in order truly to know it and to know, by experience, its meaning. *To be with the being is to know*, truly "to know" and no longer just to be informed.

The Way

Leave all dialectic behind and follow the path of the Powers; be conscious of innate functions and become *Functional Consciousness*.

Tumble with the rock which falls from the mountain.
Seek light and rejoice with the rosebud about to open:
be restless with the dog that barks in the night;
labor with the parsimonious ant;
gather honey with the bee;
expand in space with the ripening fruit;
run with the greyhound.

Be the fluid in the barrel, in the bottle, in the vase, and see if you are happy or constrained,

suffer with the sick in order to cure him, and leave behind all objective considerations.

Be function with the Power, the *Neter*.

•

To live the gesture in immobility is to evoke the gesture imaginatively. This implies having observed the gesture, and therefore sensorial information and dialectic must precede the possibility of this evocation. But this reasoning does not lead out of the restrictive circle, it is in error because based upon a cerebral conception of the imagination. If imagination were an *imaged projection* of the observed form, then the argument would be valid.

But evocation which goes beyond restrictive consciousness is a question of function and not of form. An education is indispensable here, not an education of action, but an education or, more accurately, an awakening of the faculties of functional perception. This awakening can only be produced by the momentary elimination of the *cerebral presence*, in other words of all formal representation and all dialectic of thought.

The power of fascination which many animals have is exactly of the same order, except that in their case it is a question of an instinctive action. For man, this same action, made conscious, represents the power of going beyond the limits of Nature.

Man must struggle to overcome what is the very Cause of his power: his psychological consciousness.

It is the old story of the fall of paradisal man in the Mosaic Genesis. By accepting rational Knowledge [*Savoir*] given through the complementation of man and his Eve (his shadow, his *negation*, his other "I," the objective), psychological consciousness comes to obscure functional consciousness.

It is through *Negation* alone that the light of "paradisal" union can be reborn.

To be able to deny is the only true human power, it constitutes man's free will. The animal does not know, cannot *deny*. It is the feminine aspect of man's Being—his power of negation—which enables him to rediscover Unity. And this Unity is as much masculine as feminine. Hermetically: Silver or Gold, White and Red, the two nobilities.

•

The "Power to Negate" depends directly upon *imagination*. Imagination is the faculty of retaining an image or notion and then projecting it by Thinking. Hence, it is a question of a transfer from objective, sensorial observation into

REFLECTIONS

another state which is a reflection of the object, like the reflection of an image in a mirror. This reflection becomes manipulable for thought, as the object is for the physical body. The relation of the object to its reflected image forms the psychological consciousness. The presence of the object, of which the senses inform us, cannot be denied: this object exists physically for the physical body, but its reflected image depends on our acceptance, and we can efface it by thought. Thus the Power of Negation is identified with cerebral Thinking, and determines the faculty of reasoning or the coordination of notions.

Only sensorial observation puts the exterior into *functional* relationship with the innate functional consciousness. With the development of the brain, these observations become inscribed. This forms the instrument or primitive cerebral organ, situated in the left hemisphere, the brain of memory. The right side is formed, as a reflector of the inscriptions, just as the Moon reflects the solar light.

There is a functional relationship between Thinking and this play of cosmic action and reaction, and the phases of the Moon influence the imagination.

Thus, once sensorial observation is inscribed, the reflection becomes unique to the individual, a state independent of the object and of the senses. Starting from this moment, the power of negation can be exercised, making possible reasoning, that is the manipulation, in so far as Thought, of the objective world. This allows for the transformation, suppression, and *willed schematization* of forms and appearances.

All science results from a process of elimination, disengaging truths from error. All discussion requires opposition, therefore the negation of the contrary affirmation. All intelligent observation requires comparison, which is the relative negation of one thing in relation to another. Our whole life, in Thinking as in fact, is a *combat*: a struggle through negation. The whole Universe is Action, a struggle against inertia.

Wisdom abolishes action and inertia by abolishing illusion, the reflection, the scheme, by the conscious functional identification of the In-Itself and the Outside-Itself.

•

One can make a quality appear pure by stripping a thing of what prevents it from appearing so, but it is beyond cerebral comprehension to exalt and augment this quality, because this would lead to corporeal disintegration. Qualitative exaltation is however the mystical problem posed by what the Hindu calls *Yoga,* meaning the Way of return to Unity.

To multiply Quality is synonymous with "to exalt the Being" from three-dimensional corporeal form to abstraction of form; it is, in some way, the return of the original impulsive Energy to its source. It is almost a "Spiritual Entropy."

This can only be done on the normal way through bodily death or destruction and reincarnation. Death is Nature's affair; reincarnation is a spiritual matter. It is, seen imagistically, a reiterated ascent and descent, the pendulum of incessant Life.

On the exceptional, abridged way, this is translated by a shift of consciousness into a state "beyond dimensionality," an abstraction of form, here called *Functional Consciousness.* Alternation, falling back into psychological consciousness (the acceptance of dialectics and antinomies), permits the mastery of the power to shift oneself, with ever increasing ease, into the desired state of consciousness.

There are different methods which facilitate, by means of exercises, this ascent and descent. The goal is spiritual concretization, but this time into spiritual substance: that is to say, the multiplication of Quality.

•

I do not know what Spirit is, but Spirit knows what I am, for everything is only Spirit. How can one describe in words what is perceptible neither by the senses nor by the cerebral objectivizing intelligence?

What remains, after death, of the consciousness called psychological? It ceases with the cerebral instrument. The least lesion of this organ modifies the faculties of intelligence. However, after bodily death, man does not cease to be, his material life being given over to various vegetal and animal metamorphoses, while his ashes contain an essential and fixed salt.

Nothing can stop the continuity of the being,[13] but human reincarnation can be delayed for long cycles of universal becoming. This is a sleep of the psychological consciousness: it is not a sleep of the functional consciousness.

When Spirit has received the concretizing impulse, the whole sequence of the evolution of Being is determined under one form or another of its existence. The absolute Cause of everything is this concretizing impulse I call *Functional Consciousness*. It is immanent in Spirit as the fruit is *virtually* immanent in its seed.

The sole concern of Being, when it has arrived at the human level, must be redemption. Redemption is Horian-Christic, and the gift of Christic Redemption is universal;

[13] Isha Schwaller de Lubicz, *La Lumière du chemin* (Paris: La Colombe, 1960), ch. VI.

it is the power which alone enables the surpassing of Nature. It is the Force which enables functional consciousness to awaken after the error of psychological consciousness, which is the effect of complements, oppositions, antinomies.

Redemption is the *virtuality of the Creative Word become actual*.

When this active virtuality, which is the concretizing impulse of Spirit, has transmuted the passive formative Spirit into activity, then functional consciousness will have realized all functions and will be liberated from transitory forms, which were concretized for its expression and evolution.

The concretizing Power has neither body nor form, it takes form through Spirit which gives it substance: the feminine gives body to virtuality, clothes functional consciousness with transitory appearances. These appearances must be destroyed each time that one of the functions has become conscious of itself. The Phoenix is reborn from indestructible ashes, the same being a little freer of form—if he has sought this liberation.

In sleep, one lives differently than in the waking state, but life continues. It is the same in the great sleep of form. We must learn to live beyond the cerebral illusion. This is the true prayer, the Christic awakening, the redemptive unction.

The maintenance of the thing and its nourishment are of Nature; qualitative exaltation is outside-Nature.

Procreation, which causes birth and death, is of Nature; immortality is outside-Nature.

The coupling of complements is of Nature; the magic of identification is outside-Nature.

The evolution from the virtual to the actual is of Nature;

140

the redemptive transmutation is outside-Nature.

The constant sacrifice of Osirian-Melchisedechian renewal is of Nature; the unique and absolute Horian-Christic sacrifice is outside-Nature.

Who or what, then, can tell me of what is outside-Nature, if it is not the sudden illumination and identification, or fusion, of what in myself is identical with what surrounds me?

My bones are mineral, my connective tissues are vegetal, my blood and organs are animal, my brain is human. This *coordinated* ensemble is of Nature, but this *interpenetrated* Whole is outside-Nature.

Nature is the symbolic form of what is outside-Nature.

•

Iron attracts the magnet, because they are of one another. The magnet would not be without the iron. Love.

Earth attracts the dew, because they are of one another. The dew would not be without the Earth. Love.

Woman attracts man, because they are of one another. Woman would not be without Man. Love.

Iron and magnet, earth and dew, woman and man are of Nature . . . Love is outside-Nature.

Thus to have a reason to love is not Love, to have a reason to give is not Gift; to have a reason to pray is not Prayer.

The uselessness which is imposed by Quality is the signature of nobility. And the most useless thing in the world is Gold. One cannot find the Gold of Truth outside oneself. But if you look at yourself, you will be your own enemy, as everything which is outside you is your enemy.

The "In-Itself" becoming the "I" is the fall into error, into learning [*savoir*] as opposed to Knowledge [*Connaissance*].

Identification through function eliminates dualization, puts an end to in-Itself and "outside Itself."

Let the disciple, in order to begin, close his senses and *act* by Thinking; he will discover wonders.

You do not know how to close your senses? Experience your yawn, recognize its secret. When your senses desire to close themselves for true concentration or sleep, you yawn.

I cannot say here all that gestures reveal, it is too intimate. Let your constant prayer be "The whole Work of the Universe is in me."

I put forward a pure *Individualism*, without egoism, absolute, the source of all true solidarity and of all brotherhood, for it eliminates the "you and me."

•

Collectivism is "useful," but it is of a low nature, being motivated by fear and egoism.

True solidarity is founded on the consciousness of the responsibility that every man has towards all humanity, his own kind, his species in which he is functionally based.

True Love does not require liking. To like is to recognize you and me, it is to affirm the separation. But Love is a state of union.

To awaken the Functional Consciousness is to be Love, to be Unity.

Qualification separates you from the water of the sea, from the stone, from the earth, from vegetation, from the amorous turtle dove, from the ferocious beast, from all human races; but all that appears outside of you is functionally within you, man of the end of a Time.

Qualification shows you a Moslem separate from a Jew, a Buddhist, a Brahman, a Taoist, a Christian; it discusses endlessly their "philosophies" and their merits. What is your criterion, you who do not know the revelation of Knowledge? All in their own fashion tell you the Truth, but only the Christian speaks to you openly of Redemption.

Redemption is within us, provided we awaken the Consciousness of the *function* which unifies, and renders all discussion null and void.

Is not Knowing more precious than seeking Learning?

•

A work of art is judged through indefinable "functional" communions. All "mancies" including the astrological chart are only a summons to this communion, as much in the means they employ—therefore by their functional relation to the Universe—as in their interpretation.

The authentic trance of a psychic "medium" is the state of communion of his functional consciousness with another functional state. Such a medium may be judged, for example, by making him describe the mechanism of a watch. If his functional consciousness alone is in question, his "spatial consciousness" will be different from the psychological consciousness of objective observation. He will describe the mechanism *seen from the interior*, as if he himself were "placed inside." This is difficult to fake.

The artist says, regarding his drawing: "Each stroke must be torn from the heart." This image shows how impossible it is to describe in words the state of communion which leads to the state of functional consciousness whereby "duality," antinomy, objective separation are effaced.

"A drawing, however perfect it may be, is nothing without the forceful stroke which *only the master can give it*," says a Chinese axiom.

This mastery is a gift, but one can only acquire it

through an education which awakens the highest Consciousness: will and technique are worth nothing here.

•

In these times, humanity is reaching the frontier of the possibilities which psychological consciousness confers upon it. In all domains of Thought, whether in its religious expression or in the Sciences or Humanities, *something* no longer answers to the obscure aspiration awakened by the observation of this *end* of a human power.

We seek the light in all directions when we ought, instead of seeking outside of ourselves, to return into ourselves and awaken there the state of *consciousness* corresponding to those abstractions (a kind of "logical absurdity") to which objective research has led us.

It is no longer a matter of "materialism" or "spiritualism": these are antitheses which resolve nothing; this is only a philosophical speculation which was suitable to classical Greece but becomes puerile in the face of what present humanity intuits or glimpses. Any argument can be opposed with another argument, excellent exercise for building up dialectical mental faculties; but when one has begun to struggle with imaginary magnitudes and coordinated curves, and with the geometry of the fourth dimension and with General Relativity, and when one foresees that universal gravitation may very well have nothing in common with matter such as we know it, then new faculties are necessary or else the "cerebral machine" will break down. It is the way of madness to mix two states of *consciousness* and no longer only two logics or two points of view. Ultimately, the recourse to mathematics, and even to "the multiplication of mathematics," will never be able to resolve anything regarding our knowledge of problems resolved simply by Nature before our eyes, as long as these eyes look through a state of consciousness which is not in identity with the nature of the event.

We must look within ourselves, and it is *functional consciousness* — and not *objective knowledge of function* — which is the key.

Different views of one thing, observed with one state of consciousness, form the syncretic notion of the thing. This same thing, seen from the intermediate stage above the psychological consciousness, is completely modified. The space belonging to it is "radiating" and no longer "condensed" as is that of the situated object. It constitutes a "physical void," a real center of gravity for physical bodies. *Active*, that is functional, *thinking* is of this order. We shift more often than we realize into this state of consciousness.

The first "liberation" consists of mastering this shift.

Here is the world of "fields of force," of the actions of the incorporeal, the intangible, whose *crossings* produce effects tangible for us, as a drop of acid in coagulating milk can form a solid from a liquid. The first effect of these crossings is the definition of the two energetic aspects which frame all physical matter: electric energy and magnetic energy. The one is the complement of the other, as the centrifugal equator is to the centripetal axis of a body in rotation. Cosmically, for our solar system, this constant, formative crossing is given by the solar *magnetic* force field and the *lunar* electric *reaction*. More immediately for us, Earth and Moon play similar roles.

The *physiology of the fields of forces* in the human body constitutes the description of the flux, reflux and *occult* centers, which manifest through the nervous force, the source of life, that is, through an alternate becoming and disappearing of the corporeal. These two extreme moments define what we psychologically, objectively, call Time and what I call Genesis. Momentary, corporeal specification then constitutes distance, as the passage from one specification to another is Movement.

This is a system seen through functional consciousness, but described *in the image* of psychological consciousness. It is a shift into the world of "force fields" in which objective location — objective separation — no longer exists.

•

A gesture of the hand is a movement in time, defining a distance. Physically, this *mechanical* gesture has a significance. The *significance* is functional; it is not only connected to a mental concern, but, because it is a question of a hand and not (for example) of a stick held in this hand, the hand gesture has a significance "in itself," characterized by what specifies the hand.

A fertilized chicken egg, placed in the conditions necessary for its hatching, realizes a *gesture* which we call the chicken's *gestation*. The gesture is gestating. It procreates in its corporeal aspect, because in its "functional" aspect it creates. Now to create means to make out of Nothing (the incorporeal) something corporeal to our senses.

This Nothing is the (incorporeal) substance from which everything is nourished, and "to nourish oneself" means: to extract from a material base the abstract substance which will be materialized in the nature of what is nourished, which can happen only through the destruction (digestion) of the base. Two modes for this function do not exist.

The gesture is creator, but the creature's gesture is, in its turn, the revealer of functional consciousness, a new and superior consciousness offered to the human creature, unifying the antithetical extremes.

146

The *meaning in itself* of gesture, outside of any mental or emotional attribution, is the expression of functional consciousness. This is the way in which we must understand the signature of each thing. The color of a flower is its gesture, showing the luminous, nourishing rays which it seeks: the blue morning glory summons the morning rays and the white daisy turns towards the noonday light. The *thing* obeys functional consciousness and appears to our psychological consciousness through the restrictive aspect of our senses. This classifies illusion in relation to Reality.

Psychological consciousness selects, functional consciousness unifies.

•

The Golden Number is a mathematical definition of a proportional function which all of Nature obeys, whether it be a mollusk shell, the leaves of plants, the proportions of the animal body, the human skeleton, or the ages of growth in man.

The binomial expression in algebra is a mathematical definition of a function of geometric growth.

In general, functions which preside over phenomena are the object of the study of Science, which attempts to determine their character and give them definition. But to wish to ascend to the level of function by starting from its mental, intellectual, cerebral definition is an error. To reduce functional consciousness to psychological consciousness is to descend from one stage of consciousness to another; it is a change of "world," and in order to "reascend" to the higher stage it is necessary to change the means again, just as we do in order to "descend."

We humans have acquired the power of Negation and we must make use of it against ourselves, against our mineral, vegetal and animal corporeality, through which we have acquired this supreme human power.

To renounce is relatively easy, but it is only a symbol. What we ought to do is *to deny the reality of psychological consciousness* and renounce dialectical demonstration so as to habituate ourselves to living functional consciousness. It is to let go of learning, so cumbersome and fruitless, in order to seek true Knowledge.

III. Conclusions

SPECIFICATION determines the thing completed from the "non-thing."

Specification, which is qualification in the relation of things among themselves, is functional consciousness.

When the Mosaic text declares: "God said, Let there be Light, and there was Light," the Light is a specification, and in relation to the Darkness, this Light is the *functional consciousness of Light.*

Functional consciousness is virtual activity, that is, activity immanent as possibility, which becomes actual, or determined.

As possibility immanent in the Cause, or causes, the functional consciousness is universal or undetermined but determining; Egypt calls the aspects of functional consciousness *Neters*, that is to say, Principles.

If psychological consciousness—or re-cognition of functional consciousness—enumerated the *Neters*, there would be no more *Neters* than the ones we recognize. These would be, for each epoch, the elements of a Mythology of the moment.

But history, the further back it plunges into the archaic, shows us that these same Principles have no more variation than the fixed constellations of the heavens.

We are justified in concluding that the Principles or *Neters* are not enumerated through our relative recognition of them, but by the *experimental Knowledge of a fact* which recapitulates Genesis, whether this fact be comprehensible or not.

The names change, but the *Neters* are invariable. These are the primordial Principles, not engendered but created, which are depicted without navels in esoteric representations.

This means that the Universe is created in an invariable way, which situates a continuous creation outside Time, a Present with neither past nor future.

By contrast, what is engendered continues through a birth and a death, that is, it includes an *evolution*. Evolution is the formal organization (extension) of functional consciousness, until the Possibilities immanent in the concretizing impulse are exhausted.

Concretization "descends" until the reversal of consciousness, which distinguishes man with the new faculty of Negation. From this moment begins the disintegration of the concrete. All the engendered Principles have taken a form from which they are then going to reliberate themselves: these possibilities exhausted, functional consciousness is universal.

Present humanity is only a step: the critical moment in this return to Universal Man.

Heaven, the Cosmos, has fallen face first on to the earth. In returning as Microcosmos, it comes again towards Heaven, having *known* all the sufferings of concretization, form, having become conscious "function."

This was, this is, this will be. Therefore there is conscious Creation, conscious Universe, and conscious Return of a functional consciousness. Psychological consciousness is only a transition, a relative state, situating the moment of the "reversal."

●

Creation, in other words the Present Moment, is without limit, but concretization knows a finality.

This limit is the Ego, that is to say $a : a$, as function, the thing before itself. For form, this moment is reached when the concretizing activity can struggle against all the normal environmental activities necessary for its generation and maintenance.

This same moment is vitally, definitively reached when the entire functional consciousness is concretized, formed and organized, giving each *Neter* the formal instrument of its activity.

Then the disintegration begins: organs atrophy but functional consciousness of these organs subsists.

•

Should I not call functional consciousness *Soul*? Certainly it is what animates everything, but what do we understand today by the word *Soul*, if not a symbol of an abstraction? Functional consciousness is Action, action "in itself," not what acts nor the effect of action. However abstract this notion is, it answers our concern and satisfies because it becomes factual for us by its effects and finds its sensible *image* in movement.

Accepting that the character of "specificity" can be accorded to consciousness—the notion of which is ordinarily restricted to psychological consciousness alone—allows us to conceive of different states, or stages, of Consciousness.

The effort of humanity is to elucidate the movement of things, and the progress of thought in the study of matter now poses new problems which appeal to a state of consciousness permitting the experience of function without locating the object.

Thus we pass from an arithmetic thinking to a geometric thinking of space, from Euclidian "arithmetic" geometry which has been surpassed, as has the Aristotelian syllogism, to a purely "functional" geometry.

Here again Pharaonic Egypt shows us the path by considering geometric and trigonometric functions in life and not, as the Greeks did, only in a cerebral, schematic projection reduced to lines and planes.

The cerebral schematic projection no longer answers our need today, any more than does a logical conclusion based on *imaginary* absolute terms. Each term is moving in itself. By framing our statements with "If" or "Admitting that," we burn our bridges to Knowledge, for the sake of reducing everything to a Learning based on suppositions. The most learned mathematical scaffolding rests on a reference that is "admitted" to be stable. This is always to reduce Consciousness to the lower level of psychological consciousness.

For science to become vitally fertile and to leave the material domain (which is without vital value) of mechanics, it is necessary to appeal to Consciousness and no longer only to cerebral reasoning. Until now there has been a sacrifice to the "intersubjective" truth of the group, that is to say, only what is perceived by the generality of men is recognized as true. What the isolated individual alone perceives, by grace of a state of higher consciousness or even through an exceptional sensorial sensitivity, is excluded, if not rejected, as subjective, unshared knowledge. However, Consciousness *evolves*, Consciousness is indeed the only thing to evolve; therefore we must address ourselves to the culture of this evolution in order to break the "closed circle" of psychological consciousness.

There are Functions which are concretized, coagulated in the human body, and it is divine Consciousness which is thereby humanized. Then by stages it wants to release itself from corporeal heaviness, first of all from the physical body; but it must continue its liberation, thus nothing must retain or hold it back: neither hatred, nor the spirit of vengeance, nor avarice, nor regret.

What then is this "magnet" which enables divine Consciousness to descend into the physical body and what is the *hook* which holds it there?

It is the "salt of the earth" of which the Gospels speak, the concretizing Force which from the origin made Being, and which subsists throughout all forms of concretization down to physical form. Here below it is the salt of ashes; it fixes functional consciousness, in the image of the germ, which is only the eight-hundredth part of a grain of wheat, yet will be the ear of the wheat and all the wheat in the world . . . but only wheat.

This is the "hook," and *ferment* is the connection which must be subtilized in order to make life possible in a form liberated from the terrestrial body. And we create and fashion this ferment by our real aspirations; it is he, the Being whom we must prepare, for he will be like what he must fix.

Each of us has the choice: to return to earth? or to suffer an unsatisfied call and drift in the pain of indecision, no longer able to descend and not knowing how to rise? or to pass to liberation?

We refuse to understand this inexorable reality, because we see the lifeless corpse. We forget that we look at this corpse with the senses and an intelligence which no longer belong to it, but to ourselves who are *not yet* physical corpses. During his whole physical life man obeys unreasoned impulses, which lead him on paths or towards acts decisive for his existence. He observes it later but does not accept the teaching of the fact: functional consciousness, *innate in man,* leads him to his destiny beyond all control of psychological consciousness.

The "conscious" intention of the free will? But it knows only how to break, separate, fragment what is, then rebuild with the pieces. Man is not a creator. He has one power: that of negation; it is the great gift, the gift of salvation, which is accorded him through his *fall,* but man cannot create: he can only procreate. He has the right of choice, in using his power for or against himself. His salvation consists in learning how to use it *against* himself, against his illusion, against his "I," this "I" which separates and isolates the individual from the Whole.